St. Charles College

April 28, 1953

Code of
INTERNATIONAL ETHICS

Code of
INTERNATIONAL
ETHICS

****

Compiled by
THE INTERNATIONAL UNION OF SOCIAL STUDIES

Translated and Edited with a Commentary by
JOHN EPPSTEIN
*Director and Editor, The British Society for
International Understanding and Author of
"The Catholic Tradition of the Law of Nations"*

THE NEWMAN PRESS
WESTMINSTER, MARYLAND
1953

Nihil obstat: Edward A. Cerny, S.S., D.D.
            Censor Librorum
Imprimatur: Francis P. Keough, D.D.
              Archbishop of Baltimore
September 18, 1952

The nihil obstat and imprimatur are official declarations
that a book or pamphlet is free of doctrinal and moral
error. No implication is contained therein that those who
have granted the nihil obstat and imprimatur agree with
the opinions expressed.

Library of Congress Catalog Card Number: 52–10392

Copyright, 1953, by
THE NEWMAN PRESS

Printed in the United States of America

Preface

TO THE FIRST EDITION

★★★

Some words of explanation are needed on the origin, purpose and method of this work.

According to the plan of its founders, the International Union of Social Studies devotes its attention chiefly to the study of economic and social problems in the light of Christian morality. The *Code of Social Principles* has made known conclusions which have been arrived at after several years of work. By the very nature of things, that Code had to consider various questions which come under international morality—for example, international organization of labour, regulation of commercial exchanges between States, emigration of labour, economic status of colonies. The solution of these grave problems involves a certain conception of the juridical relations between nations, and it varies with the opinion held with regard to these relations. In order not to overstep the limits of its subject, the *Code of Social Principles* had to leave much unsaid and to presuppose rather than set forth the principles of international ethics on which it based itself. This first work needed therefore to be completed.

For if Catholic ideas with regard to individual, family and civic morality are well known and need only to be mentioned briefly, the same is not true of the Catholic idea of international morality. The latter seems more

v

distant and is largely unknown even to those to whom it applies, for its applications concern chiefly the consciences of statesmen and do not ordinarily trouble that of the man-in-the-street. It therefore seemed inadvisable to take it as understood, and it appeared necessary to make a full statement of principles. The International Union of Social Studies has been true to its foundation-charter in devoting a part of its activities to the drawing up of a code published as *Code of International Ethics.*

The drafting of this Code was preceded by an enquiry into present-day methods of teaching international ethics. Leaving aside universities and theological seminaries, the enquiry considered elementary, secondary and technical schools, as well as those new types of school which have arisen in recent times: higher working-class schools for the training of trade-union leaders and schools of social service. The results of this enquiry, which covered the various European countries represented in the Union, show that the teaching of international ethics is entering more largely than ever into the curriculum of all schools of every type and purpose. In Belgium, for instance, it is an obligatory subject in elementary and secondary schools. In order to help teachers to fulfil this new task, the Belgian Ministry of Education has sent out specimen lectures which they have to explain and amplify in their classes according to the age and capacity of the pupils. There is added a bibliography giving the publications of the League of Nations, which they may consult in order to develop their explanations.

It is therefore clear that Christian teachers need a specialized manual which presents their views on international relations seriously and with sufficient fulness on all essential questions concerning those great events which nowadays go beyond the internal policy of States. One of the aims of the compilers of this *Code of International Ethics* has been to satisfy this demand. But they have also desired to do something more, namely, to give to all who wish to be acquainted with Catholic thought on the problems of international ethics, a book which, though it remains of a dogmatic and philosophic nature, makes continuous use (as the many quotations show) of the doctrinal tradition of the great theologians and the very important papal documents issued during and after the Great War of 1914–1918.

This book should not be consulted for matter which the authors have deliberately left out, for example, the rules of positive international law, the texts of treaties and agreements between States. These matters have been left to professional jurists, and the *Code of International Ethics*, though it takes them into account, claims to go beyond them. It quotes them only in order to judge them. It does not study that which exists, but that which should be. It tries to discover those higher principles to which international order must subject itself in order to win the respect of our consciences. The Mechlin Union has tried to set forth the ethics of international relations, and not compile a manual of present-day usage. It does not despise this usage, but judges it and determines the degree to which it commands the acceptance of the Christian mind.

Is it necessary to add that the *Code of International Ethics* is not the work of a Council or of the Holy See? It does not claim infallibility. Its phrases and ideas are open to discussion. But the authors do claim one merit: that of sincerity in intention and of prudence in statement.

This Code was compiled by a group of Catholics

founded by the late Cardinal Mercier, and of which his successor, Cardinal Van Roey, Primate of Belgium, is the actual President. It consists of theologians, sociologists, and students of the philosophy of law from all over the world. Each member was able freely to bring his own contribution to the common work. That in itself is a guarantee of fairness. It is difficult for any man, even though he be seeking an international ideal, to abstract from the prejudices and interests of his own country. Everyone is influenced, more or less unconsciously, by the class to which he belongs, his race, his surroundings, and is led to consider as principles of morality maxims which are current in his country, and whose purpose is merely to disguise and justify, under an apparent universality, the selfish appetites of a nation. In an international group where each member submits his ideas to the judgment of all the others, these maxims are soon shattered, and the chances of arriving at dispassionate truth are infinitely greater. Sincerity is thus checked in a manner not often found in other circumstances.

The first principles of international ethics are clear and certain. The more remote deductions from them are less so. They must be carefully expressed and sometimes corrected with a possible doubt, and one must often confine oneself to generalities which leave room for several different interpretations. Mathematical evidence is not current in the remote parts of this domain. An approximate certainty, a simple probability, or even an undecided attitude is sometimes all that one can hope for. This is not weakness, but an acceptance of facts. This prudent method will often be found in the *Code of International Ethics*. It should not be criticized on this score. It would be dishonest to give a clear outline of things which of their very nature lie in some obscurity.

M. DEFOURNY

Louvain,
July 15, 1937 [1]

[1] The Malines Union revised the *Code of International Ethics* during the years 1947 and 1948. The present edition is the outcome of this fresh elaboration. The new text was approved during the meetings which took place on September 27 and 28, 1949, under the presidency of His Eminence Cardinal Van Roey.

G. Hoyois, *Secretary*

CONTENTS

*(N.B. Arabic numerals in parentheses indicate the
numbers of the Articles.)*

****

Contents

xii

Contents

Contents

A COMMENTARY

****

This Code or, as it might be called in scholastic parlance, *Summula juris internationalis,* represents the endeavour of honest men to discover the principles and rules required by right reason, in the light of the Christian tradition, for the governance of nations in their mutual relations and in their contributions to the common good of human society. As the Preface to the first edition makes clear, it is no more than that. As one of those who took part in the revision of the Code and with the consent of my colleagues in the Malines Union, I offer the following reflections as an introduction to this English version. They are but a personal contribution to the core of it.

Popular Demand for Moral Standards

It is one of the marks of the age that public opinion as a whole demands moral standards by which to justify or condemn national acts. It was the First World War of 1914 to 1918, in which the entire population of the Great Powers and many other nations were involved in struggles and sacrifices without precedent in history, that compelled the leaders of the nations to appeal to general principles rather than to the national sentiment which had sufficed for the wars of the nineteenth century. The whole development of international relations since then has emphasized the same tendency. We have seen the first attempt to organize, in the League of Nations, a positive international society. We have known the challenge to

1

national and personal freedom as well as to the bases of world order, which the aggressions of Hitler's Germany and of Japan represented to the forces which eventually defeated them. We witness in these days the attempt to organize once more a sane and peaceful society through the United Nations—the attempt whose characteristic feature is the monstrous duel between tyranny and ordered liberty, which the threat of atheistic communism inescapably imposes upon mankind.

All these great international processes, whether good or bad, stir up instinctive judgments among simple people (which are usually sound) and discussions among the more literate of mankind (which very often are not) about what course of action in the international sphere is right and what is wrong. There is nothing more remarkable in all this than the homage which even the most rootless and unbelieving of politicians pays to the phenomenon of conscience and the reality of the natural law. Even the Communist oligarchy, which goes to great pains to deny the existence of Almighty God and of an objective moral law, cannot dispense, in its attempts to ensure the obedience of the millions whom it controls, with appeals to justice, peace and the natural virtue of patriotism. Their antagonists have to be represented as aggressors and warmongers, as enemies of the liberty and independence of nations—for that is the only language which human nature understands. If hypocrisy is the tribute which vice pays to virtue, this is the tribute which the unnatural pays to nature.

The Altar of the Unknown God

But when—apart from appeals, honest or dishonest, to natural sentiment—the rulers of this world attempt to define the *standard* by which national conduct is to be judged, we are often left with little more than question-begging slogans. We are told that the world must be made safe for democracy. But what is democracy? It is the modern altar of the unknown God. It can mean the mob rule in Italy and Germany which evolved in no time, according to the Platonic formula, into the tyranny of the Fascist and Nazi parties. It means throughout the third of mankind controlled by international communism a professed "People's Government," enforcing the blessings of socialism through the dictatorship of the proletariat dragooned by professional revolutionaries. To the secularists of the Left in the Western countries democracy mainly means a plan for material welfare for the masses organized and imposed by the State; and it is assumed that this extremely earthly paradise is a sufficient alternative to the more aggressive materialism which threatens mankind with global war. Too often also, in liberated Europe, has the term been used to whitewash the abuse of power by unscrupulous partisans. The only form of democracy which can lay claim to any moral character is the Christian democracy, which is much in evidence today in Western Europe, and exists alongside of the materialist conception, to which I have alluded, in the Anglo-Saxon lands. According to this school, to which the writer belongs, it is precisely because and only because man is a spiritual and intellectual being, created and redeemed by God and destined to eternal life with Him, that it is desirable that the largest possible number of men and women should be enabled to play a conscious and responsible part in contributing to the common good of their earthly City and, through its co-operation with other human societies, to the common good of mankind. It is on this firm ground also that the respect and defence of the fundamental rights of the human person by the State and by the international society are postulated; for that is the only condition in which the system of government by the majority can be safely envisaged. That is the one sense in which democracy—in contrast to the totalitarian State—will be found and commended in this Code.

We should, however, delude ourselves if we supposed that this is the sense in which the majority of governments and publicists, themselves committed by the unhappy practice of a century or more to the complete secularism of statecraft and diplomacy, conceive the democracy to which they tend to appeal as the ultimate good in social and international life today. It is too often the refuge of the intellectually bankrupt. As we understand it, it is undoubtedly an ideal to be pursued, chiefly by a solid work of education and with due regard to the almost infinite gradations and varieties of tradition and custom which determine the forms of national society in the world in which we live. And here we must remind ourselves that, in our search for a sure moral standard to govern mutual relations within our world society, to promote co-operation and dissolve conflicts for the common good, it is a criterion which must be applicable not only to republics but to monarchies; not only to the States of the parliamentary tradition, such as the United States, or the British Commonwealth, Switzerland or the Low Countries, but to Portugal, to Spain, to Saudi Arabia, or to the tribal society of, say, the Belgian Congo. Further, however important be the mode of electing or replacing rulers and relating citizens to the actual conduct of public affairs, all this is only a means to an end. That end is a social order which conforms to the natural law of the Creator.

Yet, if democracy is for very many the altar of the unknown God, the concept is of great value to the Christian apologist as a point of departure; it makes it possible to

4

focus attention upon individual men, their social rights and duties, and consequently upon human nature itself. And in a genuine analysis of human nature, its characteristics and its needs we discover the finger of God; so that we may say, as said St. Paul,

> It is this unknown object of your devotion that I am revealing to you. The God who made the world and all that is in it, the God who is Lord of heaven and earth. . . . It is he who has made of one stock all the nations that dwell over the whole face of the earth. . . . It is in him that we live and move and have our being . . . for, indeed we are his children.[1]

Natural Basis of Christian International Ethics

It is particularly true in the sphere of social ethics with which this work is concerned, that the strength of the Catholic tradition lies in its evoking and rationalizing what are in fact the natural needs, judgments and reaction of the normal man. That it is wrong and cruel for one State to make violent onslaught upon another; that the community attacked has the right to defend itself; that others, if they have the power, ought to go to the help of the victim of this aggression—these are almost instinctive judgments which the dreadful news of sudden war evokes from normal men, as when (in modern times) Belgium was invaded in 1914, or Poland in 1939 or South Korea in 1950. They may be misled by false or distorted information concerning the facts; but on the facts available to them, so men judge.

Observe all that is implied in these simple judgments: they confirm all that has been excogitated by the Stoic

[1] Acts 17:23–28.

and Christian moralists upon peace and war. First, there is the assumption of an objective law of justice, equally applicable to the communities which we call States and to individuals. Next, there is a distinction in the use of force—a crime if it is employed to deprive others of their lives, their homes, their liberties; a virtue if it is employed to defend these rights. Thirdly, there is the understanding of a *social obligation* resting upon governments and peoples, if they are able, to aid the injured party and defeat the unjust belligerent. But is not this a manifestation of the natural society of nations, which is the fundamental doctrine of international ethics in the Christian tradition? We might go further and notice that the condemnation of a wanton act of aggressive war—or what is believed to be such—is evidence of the ordinary man's belief that peace, a peace in which individuals and communities are free to live their own lives and gain their own livelihood, is the right and normal order of the world. It follows that war is justified only for the purpose of defending and restoring that peaceful order; further, that, owing to the evils which recourse to violence always entails, it should be the *last* resort, whereas to promote justice and resolve conflicts of interest by reasonable means is the proper and normal course for the world society, as for the national society, the local community or the family. Simple people, the world over, may not express themselves in exactly these terms or understand all their implications, but such are their convictions, as the cynical exploitation of them by the most unmoral of governments, to which I have referred, itself bears witness.

Catholic thinkers since the earliest days have in their writings on this subject followed just this practice of observing what is required by human nature itself, or rather by the laws that regulate human nature. They know that it is a fallen nature, yet one in which conscience never ceases to operate; and that since man is essentially a social being, his social relations at every stage are subject to the judgments of his conscience. They know that he needs divine grace to illumine his conscience, to subdue his passions, to enable him to follow, without aberrations, the natural law of his being. But that does not alter the fact that the proper ordering of human society can be thought out and understood by right reason, provided we start with a proper analysis of man himself.

Marxism Contrary to Nature

I lay emphasis upon this fact, for the unchristian ideology which threatens our world with ruin is based upon a fantastic caricature of man. Every heresy consists in exaggerating one fragment of the truth to the detriment of the whole. Certainly man needs material goods; certainly he is a producer or a consumer, a member of one class or another, a member of one nation or another, the subject of a government. But no one of these facts or functions explains, nor do all of them together explain, the phenomena of free will, reason and conscience, or of love, loyalty, faith, the bonds of family and friendship, the aspiration for ideals, the searching for a happiness never fully attained in mortal life. Yet such are the very warp and weft of humanity. None of these material facts explains the instinctive acceptance of the principle of sociability throughout the human race and the instinctive application of the same moral law to every part of it, especially under the impact of a sudden shock or emergency.[2]

[2] The opposite error is that of the pacifist or perfectionist, who ignores the reality and virulence of sin in individuals and groups and the fact that "law comes because of sin" and, with it, the need for enforcing law. This is a different kind of caricature of man, not so baneful in its consequences, but equally futile as a basis of human society.

7

Thus whether we arrive at the truth by deduction from first principles, after the fashion of the Schoolmen, or by a patient and objective study of human nature in the concrete, or by a combination of the two methods, we are forced to conclude that any system which denies or disregards the moral and intellectual characteristics of man, or bases itself upon the material coefficient of his nature while ignoring the spiritual, is a lie. A social structure built upon a lie cannot endure. Nature will have its revenge—that true nature created by God, to which the atheist and the materialist, while striving to enforce the unnatural, are bound to pay lip-service, because of the very texture of men's minds. That is why, in the great duel which overshadows all international life in the modern world, the natural order, safeguarded and rationalized by the Christian philosophy, is sure to prevail in the long run, while Marxist communism is doomed to frustration and failure, though the hour of doom is in the hands of God. *"Naturam expellas furca tamen usque recurret:* You may drive out nature with a pitchfork but she will always come running back."[3]

The State Is Not Absolute

It is not necessary in a Code dealing specifically with international relations to provide the detailed analysis of man's nature which is our starting point in working out the implications, on the scale of world society, of his needs, duties and rights as a social being. The clergy, teachers, seminarists and other students for whom our work is principally designed, are assumed to have acquired that knowledge before embarking upon this particular branch of social ethics. But the manner of approach

[3] Horace: Epistles.

of the Introduction and the order of the chapters are important as illustrating not only the expansion of social organization from the family to the world but also the distinction between the rights and duties of states, deduced from natural law, in an *unorganized* world and their place in a *positive international society* organized according to Christian principles.

At the start we insist that the family is a necessary and natural society of direct divine foundation, whereas other social and political groupings, with their varying power and radius of activity, are conditioned by different stages of evolution, different circumstances. Thus, while a great deal of our work is concerned with the power and responsibilities of the State (*de potestate civili*), it must be remembered throughout that there is nothing absolute in the State. The State, as Pope Pius XII has brought out so clearly in one of his wartime messages which we append to this Code (Appendix I: Christmas Allocution, 1942), exists to serve man, to safeguard the dignity of human personality, to promote the moral and material welfare of each man and woman, boy and girl, within its borders. Again, precisely because of the unity of the human race and the universality of the moral law, the State is conceived throughout as part of a greater whole, a member of the natural society of nations, to whose common good it must contribute its part. That society ordained by the Creator is a real thing, and the obligations arising from it are real and insistent, be there no man-made charter or treaty or covenant to give effect to them. None of this detracts from the high mission of civil society or diminishes the claim to obedience of legitimate authority within the State. It does, however, call in question the whole meaning of national sovereignty.

The Ethics of War in an Age of Transition

There is much in this Code which may seem old-fashioned and indeed out-of-date, and this applies particularly to the long section on war. It may be objected that to postulate the declaration of war by a sovereign government, or "prince" in the old terminology, as one of the traditional "conditions of just war" is to admit that the right of war exists intrinsically in the State. On the other hand, in a later part (Chapter Five), the use of military force to resist or repress unjust aggression is treated as a function of the organized society of nations. How can it be both?

The truth is that we are living—and this book appears—in a period of transition between two epochs.

Justification and Dangers of the State's Right of War

In a world in which a juridical form has *not* been given to the natural society of nations—we may say between the time when the Christendom of Europe and the Mediterranean lands ceased to be an accepted reality and the present day—the only means by which injury could be avenged and justice re-established in the world was by the rulers of States, acting either singly or together. War initiated by anyone *less* than the sovereign of an independent State was evidently wrong, since he was subject to an authority whose duty it was to see justice done. Only because there was no authority to whom the head of a State was subject, no superior tribunal to judge between him and his adversary, was he justified, having a just and sufficient cause, in going to war. The theologians of the sixteenth century, applying the Augustinian doctrine of war to the sovereign State as it had emerged in their day, continued indeed to surround the process of war with all the moral restrictions which twelve centuries had evolved from that doctrine. The cause must be a grave wrong done, which could not be halted or repaired by any other means. There must be a right intention—namely, to do justice and restore peace. There must be moderation in the means of war, only so much violence being used as was necessary to achieve victory; and at the end the guilty rulers should be punished but their people spared as much as possible, the peace settlement imposed being designed, not for revenge, but to preserve order for the future. War thus undertaken was regarded as an act of vindicative justice: hence the detailed examination, reproduced in this Code, of what the just belligerent may do in his judicial capacity and what, in theory, the unjust belligerent should consent to suffer.

The principle that justice between nations must be vindicated is sound enough and it was logical to conclude that, since nature—and its Author—abhors a vacuum, the only agents available to defend or restore the right must be authorized to do so; and they were the sovereigns of independent States. But, from St. Thomas onward, there crept in another and more doubtful argument—namely, that since the State was by definition a "perfect community," the government of the State must have power not only to repress internal disturbances but also to protect the community from external enemies. This seems obvious enough; but it was too easy to build up from these premises a world of wholly separate sovereign States, each having in itself "the right of war," each judge in its own cause. And that in fact is the condition of international anarchy, mitigated only by reciprocal engagements, into which the modern world developed, until the horror of the First World War in the early years of this century shocked the majority of the nations into seeking to frame, in the League of Nations, an international society to prevent war, by promoting constructive co-operation, conciliation, mediation and arbitration and, as the last resort, to authorize military "sanctions" to repress "aggression."

National Right of War Incompatible with International Authority

But there was an inherent contradiction in the League of Nations which was not the least of the reasons for its downfall. Its members retained as an attribute of sovereignty their "right of war": by convention—a revocable act of will in each case—they agreed to limit it, or to exercise it in a certain way, in the interests of the League. That was all. In the same way, they retained their full liberty of action in every other respect: the organs of the League could "request," "recommend," "advise," but not command. A minority of the States Members, by what was called an "Optional Clause," voluntarily undertook to accept in advance the judgment of the Permanent Court of International Justice in "justiciable disputes"; but these were so defined as to exclude in fact the kind of quarrels which experience shows to be the occasions of war. It may well be argued, as I myself have argued, that this approach to an organized society of the world was all that could be hoped for as a first step. Indeed, it is true enough that—however "institutional" be the organization created, in the sense that, once formed, it exists in its own right by virtue of its correspondence to natural law and the fundamental requirements of human society—it can come about in the existing world only by the process of a treaty negotiated between equals and freely ratified by them. By no other means could the Charter of the United Nations, for instance, have come into operation. Further, while all authority is from God, it is by election or consent of the persons constituting the society over which it is exercised —in this case, the "moral persons" whom we call States— that those who are to wield the authority must be chosen or confirmed in office.

Yet the fact remains that no society founded upon an antisocial principle can endure. The notion that States possess the right of war, per se, as a sovereign attribute is incompatible with the notion of an international authority having itself the right and duty to exercise or command the use of force in the service of justice. No State could survive if its individual subjects or families or local communities retained, in law, the right to use armed force, a right which they agreed to limit or delegate only by a revocable contract.

The Exercise of the Right of War, A Function of International Society

If we revert to the "parting of the ways" which, in more senses than one, the sixteenth century was, we shall observe, notably in the writings of Francis de Vittoria, a much more satisfactory justification for the power of the State to wage war—pending the establishment of a competent international authority—than the idea of sovereign self-sufficiency, overstressed and over-rationalized as it has often been by Catholic as well as by Protestant and secular authors in subsequent centuries. This is the principle that States (or princes), when obliged to make war, under the required conditions of justice, do so *on behalf* of the whole society of nations, *"en fonction de la société internationale."* [4] It is the same principle which even

---

[4] Thus Vittoria: *De Jure Belli*, 431, 19: "Princes have authority not only over their own subjects, but also over foreigners, so far as to prevent them from committing wrongs, and this is by the law of nations and by the *authority of whole world;* nay, it seems to me by natural

within civil society justifies, and in some constitutions obliges, the individual citizen, in the absence of the police, to risk his life in defending others from assault, or to apprehend a thief or murderer. We find, in fact, the conscience of mankind groping—and quite rightly groping —in this direction to justify wars of defence or intervention against what are seen to be great antisocial forces in our own times.

The people of the victorious Western Allies in the Second World War, whatever criticisms might be made of the diplomacy of their leaders or of the means employed, were almost wholly convinced that in winning the war, punishing the guilty and establishing a new world organization to preserve peace, they were acting for and

---

law also, seeing that otherwise *society could not hold together* unless there was somewhere a power and authority to deter wrongdoers and prevent them from injuring the good and innocent.

"Now, everything needed for the government and the preservation of society exists by natural law, and in no other way can we show that a State has by natural law authority to inflict pains and penalties on its citizens who are dangerous to it. But if a State can do this to its own citizens, *society at large* no doubt can do it to all wicked and dangerous folk, and this can only be through the instrumentality of princes."

The same author brings out this notion of the duty to world society of governments as just belligerents, when he treats of intervention to save human beings from tyranny in his *Commentary on the Summa Theologica of St. Thomas* (*Comm. in 40*, 1, No. 6). "If it is clear that subjects are suffering injustice from their king, it is lawful for other princes to make war upon him. And in general, when subjects have right on their side in fighting against their king, it is lawful for other princes to fight for the people. The reason for this is that the people is innocent and by natural law princes have both the right and the power to *defend the whole world lest injury be done to it* (*principibus de jure licet et possunt defendere orbem ne fiat ei injuria*)."

Thirdly, there is Vittoria's well-known passage, in which he subordinates the right of war to the superior claim of the common good of mankind (*De Potestate Civili, 13*): "Since any one State is a part of the world as a whole, and since especially a Christian province is part of Christendom, if a war is waged to the advantage of one province or State but to the detriment of the world or of Christendom, I believe that war to be unjust."

14

on behalf of the whole society of mankind. Here I am not concerned with the methods, the success or failure of these operations, but with principle and intention. The transition from war as a conflict between States to war as a function of the organized world society has, since then, been dramatically accelerated by circumstances which have not only necessitated the formation of a great military coalition, as a "regional security" arrangement in the North Atlantic area, but also, for the first time in history, direct military action by the positive society of nations itself to defeat aggression in Korea.

Laws of War and Neutrality in the Transitional Period

Before considering all the implications of these events for the development of the Christian doctrine of war, we must remind ourselves that great historical transitions, such as that in which we are now living, are not of the nature of sudden conversions or transformations. It took a thousand years for the spirit of Christianity to overcome the institution of slavery; and not until the slave trade had reached unprecedented dimensions, was it possible for popes and reformers to arouse the public conscience to the point of suppressing slavery. It is to be hoped that the abolition of war "as an instrument of national policy" will not take so long; but in a world whose component elements reveal so many stages of political development, a world in which the national right of war has so long been accepted as an institution, it is bound to be a long and arduous business.

For what has happened, especially in the last four centuries, is that sovereign States, being accepted realities and their right of war being unquestioned (even by Catholic moralists, who continued to subject it to the traditional conditions of justice), a whole body of laws of war and about war has grown up. The Church, which has seen many political institutions rise and fall or evolve into different forms, from the Roman Empire to the United Nations, has made the best of this disorganized condition of the world. She has lent her influence and authority to all that has been attempted and in fact achieved, on the one hand to prevent or end wars by the conciliation of conflicting sovereign States, and on the other to restrict the cruelties of war, as for instance by the Geneva Convention on the care of the wounded, or the Hague Conventions on the humane treatment of prisoners of war, the limitation of the implements of war, or the protection of civil populations under military occupation. All this has been built up by treaties between sovereign States and on a basis of strict reciprocity—by a process, that is, which assumes their possession of the right of war which, by a voluntary act, they either forbear to exercise in certain circumstances or exercise in accordance with certain rules. And the one moral foundation upon which all this rests, not excluding the observance of the Covenant of the League of yesterday or the Charter of the United Nations today, is the obligation to keep a promise: *pacta sunt servanda.*

This system is not only established by the habits of centuries in the sentiments of the peoples, whose patriotism almost everywhere is emotionally identified with their own national armies and navies, but is crystallized in a mass of positive law, national and international. Until the organized society of nations becomes an effective reality which has demonstrated its ability to see justice done and to use might successfully in the service of right, there may well be parts of the world where the State is fully justified in using, and therefore preparing to use, force in self-defence against unprovoked attack, and where intervention is also justified, to aid against oppression either a State so attacked or human beings. It is also quite possible that two governments equally in the wrong and equally intemperate should go to war. In such circumstances it is not reasonable to assert that neutrality, a condition recognized in existing international law, is a moral impossibility, as it certainly would be, as our Code indicates, in a world society duly organized on the right principles. It is with this very real and tenacious remnant of an older world that the bulk of Chapter Four of this Code is concerned. It is no part of the Christian moralist to make the best the enemy of the good. While the attainment of a true order for human society, conforming as closely as possible to the divine plan, must clearly be our first preoccupation in this sphere—and in our last chapter we express our strong conviction that it is the paramount duty of all who can teach or lead others to bend their efforts to that end—we must abandon nothing which can be done to uphold natural justice, to keep violence within bounds and bring charity to bear, in the imperfect, disorganized world which in fact exists, but which we are endeavouring to transform.

Unifying Stimulus of the Communist Challenge

But the transition of which I speak seems likely to be greatly expedited by the immense and unforeseen danger to our civilization which now overshadows the whole international problem. The emergence of revolutionary communism as a world power, commanding great material resources and operating an entirely new technique of aggression, in its determination to dominate all mankind, is acting as a catalyst, gradually compelling the States most conscious of its menacing character to unite in the form of a real international society, political, economic, juridical and military. Many of the cherished attributes of sovereignty are thus in the process of being sacrificed to the imperative requirements of common defence, though there are still innumerable obstacles in the form of national pride and particularism to be overcome, not to speak of internal party controversies and conflicting economic interests.

The menace of Islam to the Christian world of the Middle Ages is perhaps the only precedent for this tremendous crisis, though the terms of the contest between Cross and Crescent were different, for that was a conflict between Monotheists; and, further, those who continued to resist the Mohammedan conquests were, for all their imperfections, mistakes and recurrent rivalries, united by a common Faith and a common spiritual authority and acknowledged a common standard of law. Today the "Free World," as we are accustomed to call the nations free from the control of international communism, has, on the other hand, no religion in common. Very few States are formally Christian, though in those of European origin Christian traditions, Catholic, Protestant or Orthodox, are vigorous formative elements in the popular conscience, just as the Catholic Church and the Christian sects exercise a greater influence than is commonly realized among important Asian and African communities. Others are Islamic; others, informed by the religions of the East, Hindu, Buddhist or Confucian. A great part of the diminished Jewish community is also involved. Yet the idiom of statecraft and diplomacy for almost all States is that of the liberal secularism, which is largely the legacy of the French Revolution and has been made the language of international life by the post-Christian politicians of the West.

Such is the collection of communities with which we

have to deal and with which this Code, if it is to be of practical value, has to deal. What have these nations in common? To what common criterion can we appeal? It is to the natural law, which exists willy-nilly in the minds and affections of all men and which, unless they have deliberately denied the existence of objective morality and its Divine Author, as the Leninists have done, has a real empire upon consciences. We can now see the vital importance of the safeguarding and elucidation of the natural law, which has always been the characteristic of Catholic teaching on social ethics and international ethics in particular. Certainly the natural order is not sufficient for the Christian; but it is the proper and logical foundation of politics, and there is nothing in it which conflicts with supernatural revelation or with the sacred fraternity of Christians in the Mystical Body of Christ, of which indeed it is the necessary substructure. Yet, if that is the only logical basis or lowest common denominator upon which we can depend, we should do wrong to minimize the immense influence of Christian concepts and Christian history in the European civilization which has spread from Europe to the Americas and Australasia and, by assimilation or partial adoption, to so much of the political life of Asia and of Africa. That largely subconscious heritage is capable of remarkable revival in great emergencies —for example, the vigorous action of Catholics in the social and political life of Western and Southern Europe today, in countries almost all of which had previously been for longer or shorter periods under the domination of anti-Christian parties. And in that heritage of ideas the Crusades undoubtedly had a great formative value. It must be remembered that they extended, from the Arab conquest of Christian Egypt to the defeat of the Turks by John Sobieski before the walls of Vienna, over nearly half

of the whole Christian era. They grafted into the minds of
Christian nations the great concept of the moral duty to
unite in order to come to the aid of their oppressed fellow
men. Saint Ambrose's noble judgment, "He who does not
ward off an injury done to his fellow, if he has the power
to do so, is as much at fault as he who has perpetrated the
injury," [5] expresses a high ideal of international solidarity.
Repeated in the *Decretals* of Gratian, it became the *leit
motif* of the Crusades, upon which pope after pope elaborated. It was the historic origin of the "interventions of
humanity" which characterized the dealings of European
powers with the Ottoman Empire and much of the pagan
world until the latter half of the nineteenth century, and
is the moral basis of the process which we describe nowadays by the uninspiring term "collective security."

Transformation of the Concept of War

Bearing this in mind, let us look at the problem of war
as it presents itself to us today. What we have to fear, and
what is in fact taking place in more than one part of the
world is *not* the "war between princes" with which our
traditional authors deal. It is *not* a war which can be
exorcised by reciprocal conventions. The argument for
the mutual limitation of armaments by agreement between sovereigns, as a means of stopping the armaments
race and so reducing the danger of an outbreak—an argument so eloquently advanced by the popes of the last half
century—is largely irrelevant to the present crisis. The
group of governments which seek to dominate the world
may wear the fancy dress of sovereign States; the conventional trappings of diplomacy may be accorded to, and
unscrupulously used by, their envoys, but that is the least
important thing about them. They represent a single inter-

[5] *De Officiis.*

national force, dominated by a small and powerful group of men, fanatically attached to a doctrine which denies the moral law and the whole principle of sociability, root and branch. It attacks the whole notion of a social order based upon the natural law. It has its own elaborate formula for power which, merely as a means to conquest, uses, exploits and, when it has served its purpose, discards every sentiment, every passion, noble or ignoble, national, sectional or universal (as the desire for peace), which can excite groups of human beings against one another or weaken their resistance. Consequently the kind of aggression against which we have to provide, and which raises many new moral questions, is not at all the kind of aggression (of which military attack was the conventional type) contemplated by all our traditional Christian authorities from, say, Saint Augustine to Taparelli. Open war may indeed be used, but the characteristic forms of attack are those of confusing and antisocial propaganda; the penetration of the social structure of the intended victim; exploitation of class-hatred; strikes and industrial unrest; the steady sapping and mining of the community from within. When by any means the control of a national community has been secured, there follows with ever-increasing rapidity the suppression of individual liberties, the crushing of every rival focus of loyalty, political, social and intellectual, and in particular a ruthless war upon Christianity. Behind all this novel and highly organized antisocial aggression, operating for the most part in conditions of official peace, stand vast military forces, arbitrarily controlled by the central oligarchy, ready to step in and occupy any area which has been sufficiently "softened up," or in which, owing to the improvidence or weakness of their adversaries, there appears to be a military vacuum. They are ready also for major war, if the reactions of the free world seem to menace the Communist empire, or if it appears to be the only means which has sufficient prospects of success.

Application of Principles to New Conditions

How are the basic principles of international ethics to be applied in order to meet this total aggression against society? Taparelli d'Azeglio in a remarkable passage [6] writes:

"We have seen that the heads of subordinate societies have the right to declare war for just motives as long as the supreme authority has not attained the state of intellectual, moral and material perfection which makes it possible for it to uphold the reign of justice among these subordinate groups. In the same way, as long as the ethnarchic authority (i.e., the organized authority of the human race) is not soundly and solidly constituted, the nations may vindicate their rights by war. This imperfect state of things cannot last for ever. The ethnarchic society, like every other society, must naturally want right rather than might to prevail in its midst. In a properly constituted ethnarchy war is possible only between a refractory nation, which violates order by oppressing its neighbors, and the ethnarchic authority aided by all the peoples leagued together. In those circumstances each one of those peoples will be sure to find itself helped by all its fellow members, and will itself be organized according to the laws of the ethnarchy to which it has itself assented. It will thus be able even with quite small military forces to have perfect security concerning its own independence. It will then, as we have already suggested, no longer have to bear the enormous burden of permanent armaments."

[6] *Saggio teoretico di diritto naturale.*

We are indeed driven by necessity as well as by logic to regard war as a social process (as Taparelli foresaw), or, better, as one part of a social process operated by international authority to re-establish a right order, rather than as the act of one sovereign executing a judicial sentence upon another. If the writ of that authority runs over the greater part of the world, no doubt the use of armed force can be restricted to the comparatively easy task of constraining a single recalcitrant State. But Taparelli was wrong in his optimism. Like very many who were to develop his line of argument, he greatly underestimated the power of evil which operates against the attainment of the ideal world society, which is the logical outcome of the Stoic and Christian philosophy of natural law. What he and, after him, his spiritual heirs, the majority of the Christian supporters of the League of Nations, failed to foresee was the possibility of an antisocial force, informed with a dynamism which rejects the fundamental postulates of that philosophy, becoming as strong as the combination of States and peoples who accept it, or even stronger than these. But that is the problem of the twentieth century.

There are two great lessons to be learnt from this projection onto the vast stage of the world of the unending struggle between good and evil in the human soul. One is duly treated in this Code; the other is not fully worked out.

Universality in World Organization Unattainable

The first is that the whole presumption in favour of "universality" in the positive society of nations must be revised. Arguing from first principles and *in abstracto*, almost all Christian and humanitarian leaders of the last century—not excluding Pope Benedict XV—who have seen the organized world society as a condition of preserving peace, have assumed that all States should, when this society is formed, be admitted to it as soon as possible. Among Catholic writers, with whom Taparelli's influence has been very powerful, the line of reasoning was that, since they were all, inevitably, members of the natural society of nations, they must become members of the positive organization of that society when constituted. Some indeed went so far as to say that no government had the right to stay outside or to leave the organization.

The notion of "inevitable universality" is most cogently expressed by Taparelli in a famous passage of the *Saggio* in which he builds up, with admirable logic, from the moral and material interdependence of nations, his conclusion that a definite international society must come and must include all the nations, but subject to a qualification of which we can only now perceive the full significance. "Such is the natural development of the nations; they all tend towards a certain community of interests which must be regulated according to the principles of order and of justice. Thence comes a definite international society, in which each nation has an interest in desiring the maintenance of order. This society is the outcome of a tendency common to all peoples; and, unless nature is accidentally and violently frustrated in its proper evolution, all the nations cannot fail to come and take their place in this international society."

There is no "inevitability of progress" in this fallen world. What confronts us now is indeed a "violent frustration of nature," but by no means an accidental one. It is deliberate and it is formidable; for, as we have seen, the rulers of a great part of the world formally repudiate, by the doctrine which they profess, the existence of an objective moral law and the whole principle of sociability.

24

Moreover, they have demonstrated by their acts (over a period of thirty years and more) their consistency in this antinatural doctrine. In the newly written section of this revised Code which deals with the positive international society, we draw the conclusion that a power which flouts those two fundamental principles can have no claim to membership in the international society of which it is the potential enemy. Its admission would mean (and in the actual history of the United Nations has meant) the weakening and frustration of the international institution. I draw particular attention to the development of this point (Articles 215–222). But I would add this: it has normally been the history of political societies, that they have grown organically from smaller into greater groups. There is no reason to believe that this law is not true of the world society also. The ideal, according to our reason and religion, must evidently be an organized society embracing all mankind. But it is intrinsically probable that this will come only after bitter struggles and the overcoming of many great obstacles. Those obstacles do not, like the walls of Jericho, fall flat from the trumpeting of slogans about "One World," when, only too obviously, the world is morally torn in twain. And the first and greatest obstacle to be overcome is the presence in the world of this militant antisocial element, committed to the "total aggression" against society which we have described.

Armed Force as Part of the International Social Process

How is this challenge to be met? The practical steps to be taken belong to the spheres of politics and strategy, but the principles concerned are sufficiently clear from our tradition. The authors of this Code (see Article 47) have no doubt that, faced with this new technique of aggression by penetration, a State has the right to defend itself

25

by every appropriate means—*vi et armis,* if necessary—and that other States ought, if they are able, to come to its aid.

But that is only a negative and piecemeal approach to the problem. I would rather pose the problem thus: "Here are the majority of States committed to fulfilling their right and natural duty of bringing into being a positive organization of international society. Until this total attack upon the foundations of society is faced and overcome as a whole, there is no prospect whatever of attaining that good end. The resources of the associated States must therefore be collectively applied to a complete social process designed to overcome the attack."

Here we come to a point not fully worked out in the present Code. What is the nature of that social process? It is not merely a question of answering a particular local attack by war, in the conventional sense. The means of defending and establishing a right order must be adapted to the total and infinitely varied forms of aggression, of which military action is only one. The task is much more closely akin to the functions of the executive power in civil society than to the judicial function. To maintain order and promote the common good within the State, the police have their place and, in grave emergency, the military may be called in. But the many constructive and positive activities of government are those which minister most effectively to the prevention of disorder, by removing the opportunities of sedition. To sustain the practice and propagation of true religion, to promote a sound civic education, to pursue social justice in industrial relations, to achieve economic well-being, to ensure equal justice for all—these are the noble and necessary duties of civil government. The actual suppression of crime or insurrection is only, as it were, an exceptional corollary of this

26

normal and constructive functioning of the executive power.

So should it be in the world society; and since the contest which we are considering is as much a duel of ideas as of arms, it is of the first importance to demonstrate by acts as well as by words those principles of co-operation for the common good and that regard for the dignity of human personality which constitute the basic idea or "way of life" of our society. For instance, great international measures to raise the standard of living by economic co-operation, particularly in poor and undeveloped countries, are a vital part of the struggle against communism. Even more important would be a common endeavour to ensure, wherever the writ of the world society runs, the respect of what are nowadays called "human rights." The adoption of a common policy by the members of that society to deal with such forms of hostile aggression as the fomenting of strikes, riots and civil war is also a necessary part of the social process which we are considering. But it would be more clearly understood and would be more likely to succeed, if it were seen as the pendant of a vigorous and positive programme of social justice. Again, since the greatest potential allies of the international society in its struggle against this great anti-social onslaught are the very peoples who are held down and oppressed by the Communist oligarchy which directs the onslaught, it is essential that the purpose of the society should be, and should be *known* to be, the restoration of fundamental human rights, personal, religious, civic and social, throughout the whole world. This involves mending our ways in more than one Member State of the international society. It involves also an energetic campaign of propaganda and information, making clear in all languages and to all nations the principles for which the society of the free world stands, and which it is determined shall prevail, against the unnatural tyrannies and perversions of the enemy.

In other words, the social procedure, of which the use of military force, if judged indispensable in the last resort, is but one part, involves a total answer to a total aggression. It is an answer which requires deliberate lines of action, spiritual as well as material, in the fields of politics, economics, industrial relations, popular education and diplomacy, as well as military strategy.

Armed Force,
An Executive, Not a Judicial, Function of World Society

If military force is used to resist actual attack by the adversary or as the only means of defeating the antisocial aggression, it is an *executive act* of the world society, which must be judged by the same canons as those which govern the use of physical force by the police or army within the State. The amount of force used (in the international sphere this includes the choice of weapons) must be proportioned to the actual violence done or immediately threatened by the enemies of order. In civil society, if a small number of rioters can be dispersed by a mere show of force or by the police apprehending a few ringleaders, it is not justifiable for the police to fire on the crowd. If, however, shots are fired by the rioters or if they attack life and property, then it may be necessary, and therefore right, for the forces of order to use firearms. If actual sedition or civil war starts, force must evidently be employed to suppress it; and it will be the duty of the government, as far as possible, to limit the area of the trouble and to use the minimum of violence consistent with the vigorous restoration of order.

These are the principles which, on the world scale,

must determine the use of the new and terrible atomic weapons. The two schools of thought upon the legitimacy of employing any instruments of mass destruction are candidly set out in this work (Article 170b). Evidently the wholesale massacre of the very human beings whom the world society intends to liberate defeats the whole moral purpose of its coercive action. No lesson of the Second World War is more disturbing than the progressive sacrifice of the end of war to the means of war which, under the impulsion of demagogy, characterized the policies and military methods of the victors in its latter stages. It must never be said of the Christian soldier and statesman "Where they make a wilderness, they call it peace."[7] They must never cease to remember that "war is waged that peace may be attained; therefore, even while warring you must be a peacemaker, that by defeating those against whom you are fighting you may bring them back to the values of peace."[8] This fundamental rule governs those engaged in "police action" on behalf of the organized world society even more obviously than it does sovereign States engaged in war in the old sense. Subject to this overriding principle and the intention never deliberately to kill innocent people, so much violence and such weapons may be used as are really necessary to victory; the decision largely depends upon the actual military strength of the antisocial adversary and the implements of destruction which he employs.

Once war is seen in its true perspective as part of this social procedure as a whole, namely, as a police action undertaken by the executive organ of the world society

[7] Tacitus: *Agricola,* 30, *"Ubi solitudinem faciunt, pacem appellunt."*

[8] St. Augustine: *Ep. ad Bonifacium,* 189, VI, in the light of which the reader could do worse than contemplate the thoughtful little book *Great Mistakes of the War* by H. W. Baldwin.

as a necessary means of defeating what is, in effect, an insurrection on the grand scale, there are many particular problems which will fall into place.

First of all, we can see the fallacy latent in the old notion of war as a judicial act. It is a fallacy, not because it is unnecessary in certain circumstances to vindicate justice by force, but because of a confusion of functions. Judgment is by its essence an independent intellectual act. The sovereign State involved in a conflict with another cannot, by the nature of the case, be an independent judge. A policeman is not a judge; neither is a soldier. True, in the Christian tradition, they are justified in killing or wounding, damaging or destroying, only if they and those who legitimately command them are acting in honest pursuit of justice. But that does not necessarily mean the execution of a particular judgment. It may equally be (and within civil society almost always is) the fulfilment of a standing or permanent mandate, namely, to maintain law and order or "keep the peace." And there is no mandate more imperative than the achievement of a right social order in the world, an order which conforms to natural law and morality and promotes the common good. Once a positive society of nations has come into being as an institution to achieve that end, its executive authority necessarily possesses that permanent mandate. The military actions of individual governments, which have been justified potentially hitherto as operations undertaken on behalf of the whole society of nations, now come actually under that mandate. If forced, in this transitional stage of the world, to act separately in a sudden emergency, such as resistance to external attack or armed rebellion initiated by the enemy of society, a government finds its duty and its justification as the agent of the whole society, upon whose collective aid it has the right to count.

Some Particular Problems
(i) Ultimate Purpose of Resort to Armed Force

What, then, of the *object* of war, in the sense of coercive or police action undertaken as a social procedure by or on behalf of the society of nations? Is it right (as many contemporary politicians are in the habit of suggesting) that it should always be purely defensive, in the sense that it has no application to what is happening in the lands at present overrun or controlled by the antisocial power with which we are confronted, but is solely concerned with repelling attacks upon those areas which it does not as yet control? I reply that such a position is as unmoral as it is selfish. Justice is the same the world over. The rights of God, of His Church, of individual human beings, of families and of the groups which they form because of their varied spiritual or material needs, are the same in Poland or in Hungary or in Czechoslovakia, and indeed in Russia or China, as they are in the United States or Canada, France or Britain. And it is precisely to defend those rights and achieve an order in which they can be duly exercised, that the formation of the organized international society is justified. The fact that these fundamental rights and liberties have been and are being outrageously violated means that, if force is employed to put an end to that violation, it would not in any sense be a "preventive war": it would be war or police action, defensive in origin, and of just intervention.

But here the very real virtue of prudence must be considered. Neither rebellion nor armed intervention is justified, however good the cause, if there be no reasonable prospect of success or if the harm likely to be done is out of proportion to the good to be attained. The decision in this case depends purely upon an accurate appreciation

31

of facts; but there should be no question that the complete defeat of the antisocial power, and with it the liberation of the oppressed populations, should be the ultimate aim of the world society.

(*ii*) *The Question of Resistance Movements*

The same counsels of prudence determine the answer to the question whether it is right to initiate or encourage resistance movements in countries subjected to Communist rule, or in any others that may be unjustly occupied by the enemy. The section of this Code concerned with the position of the civil population of a country under the military occupation of an unjust belligerent provides the guide to an answer (Article 178b). Objectively, the population has no duty of obedience to an unjust occupying power and, in the case of a tyrannous government arbitrarily imposed upon it, may have just cause for armed rebellion. But unless such a resistance movement is likely to achieve its purpose without causing frightful reprisals, unless it is judged to be an essential contribution to the campaign of the international society against the oppressor, and unless society can furnish prompt and powerful aid to the rising, it would be contrary both to charity and to justice to initiate or stimulate it.

Immense harm was done both to the principle of legitimate authority and to the national unity of the countries concerned during the Second World War by the reckless encouragement of the resistance movements, despite the heroic individual sacrifices made by individual partisans, because almost everywhere they developed into civil wars.

That was, no doubt, a particular case from which it would be unwise to generalize. Legitimate governments of many of the occupied countries were in exile and, though in no position to contribute decisively to the defeat of the enemy, progressively gave their authority to measures of sabotage and violent resistance, without full regard to the consequences, partly to justify their position as the allies of major belligerents, partly in the hope of preventing the natural resentment of the population in occupied territory which was being exploited by their own political enemies. On the other hand—and this was the decisive factor—it was the known deliberate policy of the Soviet Government to stir up and exploit "national liberation movements" with the object of promoting social and political revolutions in favour of communism. They very nearly succeeded, and in the process, caused damage to the social structure which is humanly irreparable, especially in France. It is not easy to forgive the culpable blindness of the leaders of the Western Allies in this regard, for it went far to compromise the essential justice of their cause.

The problem would be different in the case of a war undertaken by the society of nations to restore national and international order against antisocial revolutionaries. But, apart from the general dictates of prudence which we have outlined above, no good can come of disregarding more than is absolutely necessary the distinction between guilty and innocent, military and civilian, so painfully built up by the Christian spirit over several centuries, with the constant object of restricting to the minimum the impact of armed conflict upon human communities. Further, even in warring against an unjust revolutionary government, the danger of favouring conflicting factions when fomenting underground war will always be present. The old principle that acts of war can justly be commanded only by the competent authority loses none of its validity. We insist in this Code that all departures from the rule of passive obedience on the part of the civil population, while the issue of war is being decided by regular armed forces, must be disciplined and authorized, a condition difficult to fulfil as long as legitimate and duly recognized governments do not exist, even in exile.

(*iii*) *Laws of War in International Police Action*

This brings us to the application of the laws of war in general in a conflict resulting from the use of military force by the organized world society in order to defeat the challenge of antisocial aggression. The most serious objection to the thesis which I have advanced is that, by not treating the enemy as a recognized belligerent, but rather as a rebel against whom society through its executive powers takes "police action," it destroys reciprocal arrangements, in the functioning of which neutrals have played a beneficent part, to keep war within certain bounds. There are conventions not to use certain weapons (e.g., poison gas and bacteriological warfare); to respect the immunity of the Red Cross; to treat prisoners of war in accordance with a prescribed code and return them to their homes at the conclusion of hostilities; and so on. What will happen to them?

The answer to this objection is that the system has been destroyed already, not, of course, in the case of an armed conflict between civilized States as such, which may still unhappily occur, but in the case of that great world contest which we are considering. The police do not make conventions, on the basis of reciprocity, with burglars or murderers or armed rebels; and, in any case, it is impossible to make conventions with a power which accepts no obligation to keep a promise. In point of fact, the Soviet Union does not hold itself bound by the Hague Conventions, with the result that for the first time after a major war, since the evil practice of enslaving prisoners was generally abandoned, hundreds of thousands of unfortunate men, Japanese, Germans, and Italians, if they have not died in captivity, remain subjected either to forced labour or to indoctrinization, to be used as the agents of their conquerors against established authority in their own countries. The commanders of the armed forces of the international society should never disdain any temporary or local truce or bargain with the adversary, as, for instance, the exchange of wounded prisoners who desire repatriation, if by these means even one human life can be saved, even one family reunited. At a stage when the international society is still embryonic—as it now is—it may not be strong or united enough to achieve victory in a particular area; its representatives may therefore be obliged to make a local composition with the enemy.

But it is evident that with such an antagonist it is not possible to fulfil the purpose for which the laws of war have been constructed, by means of a convention which has much prospect of being observed.

This does not mean that the forces operating on behalf of the lawful international authority are in the slightest degree dispensed from all the prescriptions of moderation and mercy with which Christian civilization has surrounded the use of might in the service of the right. The police in civil society are ruled by many restrictions regarding the respect of life, liberty and property and are forbidden to use cruel or arbitrary measures, because they are, and must be trusted to be, the agents of justice. So, *mutatis mutandis,* it is of the utmost importance that the commanders and soldiery of the world society should exhibit, not only in the conduct of military operations, but in their behaviour to the civil population, the discipline

35

and humanity which are required by the noble cause
which they serve.

(iv) An Objection Answered

In commending these thoughts to my fellow students
of the moral questions raised in international life by the
tragic but epoch-making developments of our own days, I
am conscious of the criticism that pure theory in regard
to the ethics of war has been confused by being considered at every point in relation to concrete circumstances.
The proposition which I have advanced—namely, that the
use of military force, outside the confines of a single state,
is to be justified as part of a social procedure set in motion
by, or on behalf of, the executive authority of the
organized society of nations—is coloured, it may be said,
by the particular, temporary menace of world communism
on the one hand, and, on the other, by the existence of the
United Nations. In the same way, it may be argued, the
earliest Christian moralists rationalized the war of their
own times, which was mainly the defence of the Roman
Empire against the barbarian; or the theologian of the
Middle Ages, the Crusades against Islam; or Vittoria, at
the beginning of the Colonial Age, the impact of the
Spaniards upon the backward peoples of the New World;
or Suarez, the practice of war between independent
sovereigns as he knew it; or the popes of the last century,
the practical means of bringing under control the competition in armaments and national ambitions between the
powers.

My answer would be that there is no pure theory of
war. We start from, and we return to, the simple proposition that in human society, because of sin, material force
is, on occasion and as a regrettable necessity, required by
natural law as the servant of justice. By whose authority

and within what sphere it should be employed, depends upon the practical dangers which have to be met and the stage which has been reached in the political evolution of mankind. But the very fact that the lawful use of force is governed by universal principles creates a pre-supposition in favour of the view that it is potentially, at least, a function of the whole society of the human race.[9] Reread, without regarding the superstructure of the intervening centuries, the judgments and counsels of those great minds, St. Ambrose and St. Augustine, upon men's duties in regard to peace and war, written in the dawn of the Christian age, when, steeped in the finest achievements of the ancient philosophy, they were considering in all its freshness and sharpness the question of how the conclusions of human reason and the implications of Christian revelation should be integrated. One cannot fail to be struck by the fact that their conclusions, though prompted by the circumstances of their age, are invariably of general application; there is no suggestion that they refer only to this nation or to that; they relate to the common good of all men. St. Augustine, Roman as he was to the core, extends his vision in the *De Civitate Dei* far beyond the crumbling bastions of the Empire he loved to the peace of the whole world, and leaves us the best of all definitions of peace, in terms of the ordered relationship of men and human communities to one another and to God. There can be little doubt that the exercise of

[9] The true nature of war as an international, social process is shown in the admirable *Essai sur l'Ordre Politique National et International* by Mgr. Bruno de Solages and Father J. T. Delos, O.P. (Paris: Librairie Dalloz, 1947), and has been elaborated by the latter author in his articles "The Dialectics of War and Peace" in *The Thomist* (Baltimore, Maryland: The Thomist Press, July and October, 1950). In this essay I carry the theory a stage further, testing it by the exigencies of the actual situation created by the challenge of communism to the international order.

armed force, when it is unhappily needed, by the organized society of nations accords best with these fundamental and early teachings. The notion of a right of war inherent in separate sovereign States was at best the rationalization of an anarchic condition of human society, resulting from the failure of the noble attempt to give the Christian world both a temporal and a spiritual unity; it was somewhat uneasily justified by a formula of substitution for the non-existent superior international authority. Only when a positive organization of the natural society, however imperfect, is actually in existence, is it possible to give practical form to the universal principle in regard to the social character of physical coercion; but it is possible, and right, I believe, to deduce it from the primacy of the common good of the natural society of nations over the good of the parts.

Conclusion: Providential Purpose in World Crisis

Insofar as this conclusion is provoked by the unprecedented danger to the whole basis of the social structure which the powerful forces of world revolution represent, we must not forget the hand of Providence in this development. Such are the limitations of the human mind, so deep the sectional prejudices, and so powerful the habits formed by immediate material interests, that great political federations or unions have hardly ever come about in human society except as the result of some imminent menace. Humanly speaking, the challenge of aggressive materialism to the natural order of society, informed by that primacy of the spiritual which is the characteristic of the Christian civilization, was bound to come, though no one could have foreseen its magnitude. Qualified as it is by the national characteristics and inhibitions of that great nation which the Marxist revolutionaries first conquered, it yet bears the marks of its origins—the revolt against authority, spiritual and temporal, and with it the rejection of the supernatural origin of authority, by the French Revolution; the idolatry of the "sovereign people"; the Liberalism of the new industrial age which gave birth to the notion of blind economic laws; the class war with which, in a dechristianized society, nineteenth century capitalism presented the embittered agitator. This is not the place to describe the many stages by which, especially by the Prussian methodism of Karl Marx, the semblance of an imposing theory of inevitable world revolution, to be precipitated in the interests of "the workers," was constructed upon the basis of a collection of false and partly false premises. The striking successes of revolutionary socialism in the succeeding years and its attraction for the "intelligentsia," or rather semi-intellectuals, who have used it to capture "the masses," lies in its offering to those who have lost faith in the supernatural and with it their understanding of nature itself, a new and spurious religion or philosophy of life. It is this fanaticism, with its blind obedience to new absolutes, its fatal attraction to those sinister qualities—envy, jealousy, hatred, material greed and ambition—which are latent in all of us fallen men and are most inimical to ordered society, which gives communism its particular virulence today. One man, it is true, has given it a new character as a highly developed and cynical formula for power, so that in the international field it is for practical purposes identified with the armaments, material resources and diplomacy of Soviet Russia and the other countries which come within his orbit. But that does not alter the fact that it is in the spiritual and intellectual order that its chief danger lies; and on that field it must be met and fought. For all the false ideas and evil or per-

39

verted human motives which have gone into the making of this great enemy of the true religion and of human society, are present in one degree or another in the various parts of the international community, which is now impelled in self-defence, and in great confusion of mind, to oppose it. How much selfishness, how much materialism, how widespread a denial of God in practice if not in theory, how blind an idolatry of popular sovereignty, how shocking an absence of any sound moral philosophy is to be found everywhere in the free world, as we call it! Not by these means, nor yet by a superficial overlaying of our national and sectional divisions by a vague humanitarianism or by what may be described as post-Christian sentimentality can we hope to stem the great attack. Hard thinking and hard searching of conscience are required. It is by uncovering that great God-made bedrock of the natural law that we may hope to show the honest, normal man how his deepest needs and instincts fit into a reasonable plan for the ordering of the world.

It is a coherent philosophy of life that he needs to oppose to the false faith of communism. If he is to make sacrifices of his goods and liberty and even of life itself, it must be for principles which appeal to his moral nature and for a scheme which makes sense to his mind. This, in the sphere of international life, as in that of the nation and the city, the family or the factory, Catholic social doctrine provides. For it is not the least of the glories of the Church that for so many centuries she has guarded and elucidated the natural law, applying it to the changing needs of human society, enlightening men's minds and firing their wills with the supernatural motives which the Christian revelation alone provides. It is in the belief that this little book is a not unworthy continuation of that great tradition that I humbly offer this translation of it, and with it, for what they may be worth, these personal reflections, to my fellow students in the English-speaking countries.

JOHN EPPSTEIN

Benjamin Franklin House
    Craven Street
        London, England
            Maundy Thursday, 1951.

A CODE OF INTERNATIONAL ETHICS

INTRODUCTION

****

1. Ethics may be defined as the science of the principles which direct human activity to the integral good of man. It establishes the rules and precepts to which his conduct must conform if he is to attain his ultimate end.

2. This science of ethics falls into two parts—general morality and special morality.

The former considers that which is universal and permanent in human nature and thence deduces the general laws which govern every form of human activity.

The latter envisages man in the concrete and contingent conditions of his existence, conditions in which his activity is diversified according to the immediate aims in view and the particular fields of action. Hence we are led to classify special morality as domestic, professional, civic or social, and so forth.

Among these different branches of special morality comes international ethics. This is the moral science which governs the conduct of men and, more especially, of rulers, in their international relations.

3. There are many people nowadays who deny that politics, whether international or national, are subject to the empire of morality. Starting with a false conception of the sovereignty of the State, they admit no limit to its independence other than it may agree to place upon itself.

According to this notion, the State creates unto itself its own standard of justice and honesty, to serve its own interests.

The Christian conscience will always reject this insolent pretension, which substitutes arbitrary power for the right and leaves the door wide open to every tyranny. "That which is not permitted in private life is no less prohibited in public life." [1]

All societies are composed of human beings; they are governed by the exercise of free will; they are, then, in the true sense, moral persons as well as physical entities; and they are subject to the moral law, by whose sovereign authority every human will is governed. The mutual relations between societies are therefore regulated by a number of rules and precepts which constitute international morality.

4. Grounded in human nature, these rules and precepts give expression to the most wise and just order established by God Himself for the prosperity of the peoples and the true happiness of mankind.

[1] Leo XIII: Encyclical *Longingua Oceani,* 1895.

* 1 *

HUMAN SOCIETIES

****

I. FAMILY, CITY, STATE

5. Men are descended from a single couple, their first parents; they are children of the same Father, who is in heaven; they have been redeemed by the blood of the God-Man and are invited to incorporate themselves in His Mystical Body. Mankind therefore constitutes a single family; and no differences of race, colour, language or nationality can hide the indestructible unity of that family.

Natural morality, confirmed and reinforced by the law of the gospel, creates reciprocal duties of justice and charity for all human beings in their relations with one another. Among other things, it puts them under an obligation to contribute, each according to his means, to the establishment and maintenance of material and spiritual conditions favourable to the full development of the human race and conducive to the common good of mankind.

6. Each individual can indeed contribute directly to this common good—for example, by the spreading of sound doctrines, by discoveries in the realm of science, and especially by the graces which his prayers and merits obtain for the human race.

44

Normally, however, this influence extends only to a very limited circle, and it is only through a system of relationships of ever-growing complexity—families, township, profession, State—that it eventually affects the human race as a whole.

7. Man, being incapable of obtaining alone all that is necessary for his existence and development, is naturally led to seek in the society of his fellow men those things which he lacks.

The family is his first and most firm support. But families themselves are bound, in order to secure for their members all the things which their nature demands for their betterment, to unite into a larger group: the city or State. The State also unites and governs other natural or voluntary groups which are formed to promote certain specific common interests, either cultural or professional, scientific, artistic, and so forth.

8. Every society is formed for the common good of its constituent members; the family, in its limited sphere, seeks the general good of its members: the other subordinate societies pursue some specific interest. But neither is called upon to secure for its members all the conditions required for a truly human existence. It is the purpose of the State, which unites them all in a higher unity, to provide those general conditions which will enable each one to attain more easily "the full good of human life" (St. Thomas). For this reason it exercises sovereign power over the territories under its control.

II. Collaboration Between States

9. In spite of this legitimate sovereignty, the State finds itself more and more bound up with similar groups into which the human race is divided, in strict relations of interdependence, without which it would be unable to

accomplish its task. The "full good of human life" which the State must give to its members cannot even be thought of apart from a wide sharing in the material and spiritual life of the whole world, as well as in the varied resources which the Creator has scattered all over the globe.

But this sharing is possible only if all States mutually assist one another in establishing an international regime which will enable all to fulfil their functions adequately. States are therefore bound, by the very nature of their mission, without losing their own individuality and legitimate authority, to belong to a higher group—international society, or the society of States—which finally establishes the human family as a well-ordered organism, capable of lasting and full of wonderful possibilities.

10. The family, political society and international society—*domus, urbs, orbis,* as St. Augustine has it—are institutions of natural law, since they correspond to certain fundamental needs of human nature. But as regards their actual constitution, they have not always been equally necessary and have developed successively in the course of ages.

The family is as old as the human race. It could not have been otherwise, since the family is at once the source and the preserver of life.

Various needs, such as the maintenance of order and security, collective works, and so forth, soon led families to unite on a more or less extensive scale into cities and States entrusted with the management of the common good of all the associates.

11. International society has been a much longer time in taking shape. The peoples of the earth, having fallen from the state of original justice into barbarity, separated also from each other by more or less insuperable natural

barriers, by differences of climate, language and customs, had forgotten their common origin. For long centuries men considered the stranger merely as a harmful being—*homo homini lupus*—and fought him without mercy. But at last the imprescriptable law of nature triumphed over the worst barbaric instincts. It began by submitting war itself to its dictates. Later the need of securing even elementary security made relations between nations more peaceful. The spread of the gospel message of brotherhood and love, the progress of civilization, the economic development of all the continents, the improvement in means of communication, all these things have powerfully contributed to remind nations of their close solidarity. Today no State could adequately fulfil its mission without the individual or collective assistance of the other members of international society.

12. For a long time the fact that nations were widely scattered and consequently lived in isolation prevented any considerable and fruitful international collaboration from taking place, and philosophers and moralists alike came to consider the State as a *perfect society,* endowed with all the necessary means to help its members to attain "the full good of human life."

Things are very different today. In view of the great extension of international life, the term *perfect society* can be applied to the State only in a very restricted sense.

The State is still a perfect society inasmuch as it possesses full authority to maintain order, peace and justice within its boundaries, since a universal State which could claim immediate jurisdiction over all members of the human family is almost unthinkable.

But the State is no longer a perfect society inasmuch as it cannot now give to its subjects, by its own means, the "fullest good of human life," such as the progress of civilization and the fruitful resources of an harmoniously organized international co-operation have rendered possible.[1]

III. THE NATURAL SOCIETY OF STATES

13. In fact, the same law of sociability, which impels individuals to seek in mutual aid the indispensable complement of their own inborn weakness and needs, obliges States to require close and continuous collaboration with other States, as the means of fulfilling their purpose in regard to their own subjects.

14. Every society is constituted for a common good, in the attainment of which all the associates are interested and bring their individual contribution. The common good to which the co-operation of nations must tend has a twofold object:

(a) The maintenance of international order, which will enable each State, enjoying the full posses-

---

[1] This new interpretation of the "perfect society" can claim the support of Pope Pius XII, who wrote in his encyclical *Summi Pontificatus,* October 20, 1939: "Indeed the human race, though divided, in virtue of the natural order established by God, into social groups, nations and States, independent one of another, as far as concerns the organization and regulation of their internal life, is nonetheless united by mutual bonds, moral and juridical, in one great community, which is ordained for the good of all nations and governed by special laws that protect its unity and develop its prosperity. Who, then, does not see that to assert the absolute autonomy of the State is to oppose outright this immanent and natural law or, rather, to deny it root and branch, putting the stability of international relations at the mercy of the rulers' will and removing any possibility of genuine union and fruitful co-operation in the general interest?"

Such also was the view of Suarez, who wrote in his treatise *De Legibus ac de Deo Legislatore* (Ch. XIX, No. 9): "If each State, republic, or kingdom constitutes a perfect community in itself, it is nonetheless true that since these communities cannot suffice to themselves in isolation, they must maintain one with another certain relations of mutual assistance and society, for their own good and for their own development."

sion of its rights, peacefully to attend to its social tasks.

(b) The progress of civilization by the exchange and inter-communication of material and spiritual wealth. International institutions which make up for the inability of single States to direct their efforts in harmony for the greater good of the collectivity (transport, hygiene, suppression of immorality, labour organization, intellectual co-operation, commercial exchanges) will further such progress most effectively.

15. As a collective entity, international society can live and act only through the work of its members. The latter have a right to its help and services, and in return they are obliged to co-operate efficaciously, according to their means, in the work from which they derive so many benefits. International life will be active and fruitful precisely inasmuch as the various States appreciate the natural solidarity which unites them and agree to comply with all its conditions.

There can be no social life without self-abnegation and sacrifice. The States, as members of international society, will have to subordinate their special interests to those of the collectivity and submit their independence, as far as is necessary, to the law of the international community.

16. This necessary subordination of national interests to the overriding interest of the whole family of nations will be achieved only if each State succeeds in overcoming the selfish appetite and insatiable cupidity which Saint James the Apostle denounces as the primary cause of all conflicts.[2]

---

[2] "What leads to war, what leads to quarreling among you? I will tell you what leads to them: the appetites which infest your mortal bodies. Your desires go unfulfilled, so you fall to murdering, and you cannot

17. On the other hand, States must cease to claim that absolute independence which nature has not given them and which in fact they have never possessed. Their rights are exactly proportioned to the mission of protection and assistance which they exercise in regard to their own subjects. They cannot efficaciously fulfil their mission alone, without the help of international society and outside its framework. They can command with sovereignty within their own frontiers, but must submit their authority to the higher and necessary law which ordains all national activities to the common good of humanity.

18. These sacrifices will naturally hurt the self-esteem of nations and rulers. But they are necessary, and will eventually turn to the advantage of those who accept them. For as the individual "fully becomes what he has the right to be only when he ceases to think of himself alone," [3] the State can effectively fulfil its mission only when, looking beyond the narrow circle of its national interests, it agrees to collaborate wholeheartedly in the common tasks of international society.

In helping to maintain international order, it provides as much as and even more than by armaments for its own security; and in promoting the cultural and economic development of other nations, it labours for the prosperity of its own subjects.

19. International society fulfils the innermost tendencies of human nature. These tendencies do not become evident or compelling until the progress of civilization has

---

have your will, so there is quarreling and fighting" (James 4:1–2). Pius XI develops this theme when he writes about earthly goods in his encyclical *Ubi Arcano Dei* (1922): "Being very limited, unable to satisfy everybody equally or to provide anyone with his full requirements, they become, for that reason, the sources of discord and animosity."

[3] A. Valensin: *Semaine Sociale du Havre,* 1926.

created between nations a bond so strong that to return to original isolation would cause grave damage to themselves and to the rest of the human community. Henceforth the nature of the duty of nations towards international society changes. Previously it was of a purely negative character, forbidding any State to oppose directly the constitution of such a body; it now becomes a positive duty, and compels nations actively to co-operate in the common task of order and civilization under an international authority.

20. Every society in fact requires an authority, whose task it is to co-ordinate the activities of its members in view of its proper end, which is the common good of all the associated persons. The community of nations is no exception to this fundamental law of social life: no less than other societies, it postulates an authority to govern and guide it, in all that is necessary for its existence, towards its own perfection and its appointed end.[4]

21. "Authority comes from God only, and all authorities that hold sway are of his ordinance." [5]

The constituted authority of international society proceeds from the same source, and has therefore a right to command the respect of all the associated States. The Creator, however, has left to man the task of elaborating the structure of this authority and the forms of its exercise.

22. In principle there is nothing to prevent men from conferring this authority on one person or a small group. In the Middle Ages the great family of Christian nations had tended to this when it was placed under the double jurisdiction, spiritual and temporal, of pope and emperor.

In point of fact, however, this semi-monarchical solution did not prevail. Schism and heresy soon detached

---

[4] Taparelli d'Azeglio: *Saggio teoretico di diritto naturale,* No. 1364.
[5] Romans 13:1.

great and powerful nations from their allegiance to the Holy See, and kings and princes, anxious to secure their independence, disputed the primacy of the imperial crown, and for a long time even the idea of an international society was forgotten.

23. This society, nevertheless, continued to exist in law and in fact, and this existence postulated an authority. The law of nations (*jus gentium*) has not ceased to govern international relations. But how can one conceive of a law of nations, that is a body of laws binding upon all nations, unless there exists a real authority qualified to promulgate these laws?

Consequently, so long as no particular person (or body) has been invested with the international authority, it resides in the common accord of the associated States, and it is for them to determine in what forms that authority is to be exercised.[6]

24. The rights and duties of the international authority are naturally determined by the very end of the society of States.

The first and principal duty of this authority is to secure for its members, together with the inviolability of their territory, their legitimate independence and the full enjoyment of all their rights.

Secondly, it must positively assist the progress and improvement of the associated nations by putting at their disposal those institutions and collective services which will enable each one to attain more efficaciously its own end.

[6] "The law of nations does not derive its binding force simply from a human convention; it really has the force of law. . . . No kingdom has the right to refuse it allegiance, for it has been established by the authority of the whole universe" (Vittoria: *De Potestate Civili*). See also Taparelli: *op. cit.*, No. 1366.

25. The international authority can fulfil this protective and constructive mission only with the help of the associated States. It has therefore the right to claim their assistance in order to ensure the maintenance of international order and the respect of justice, as well as to found those institutions of collective utility needed for the progress and improvement of the human community.

26. To this right of the international authority corresponds the duty, on the part of the rulers of the associated States, to respect its commands in all that concerns the common good of the society of nations, as well as to collaborate with it generously and faithfully. None has the right to disobey its orders unless they overstep the natural boundaries of its jurisdiction or constitute a manifest violation of justice.

No State can be allowed, under pretext of safeguarding its independence, to forswear all allegiance to international society. This gesture would not suffice to destroy the natural fact of solidarity which unites it to the family of nations and obliges it to contribute to the prosperity of all.

27. In any given political society individuals are allowed to form smaller groups, the purpose of which does not contradict the superior end of the national community. Likewise the various members of the international community can establish particular agreements, leagues or alliances with a view to attaining certain reasonable ends compatible with the common good of the universal community.

But in order to prevent the necessary unity of the universal association of peoples from being broken up, anything which would make these groups or regional agreements appear to be directed against any other State or group of States must be carefully avoided.[7]

28. Such are the principles of that international society which is postulated by the very nature of man; the task is now to translate it into acts and to realize it effectively. It is an extremely delicate enterprise which requires the co-operation of all men of good will, both rulers and ruled. Catholics have no right to stand aside from this task. It is to help them to form a right judgment in the study of these grave problems that this effort has been made to condense into a Code of international ethics the principles and conclusions of Catholic sociology. Thus the following chapters deal in succession with the essential rights and duties of States (Ch. II); relations between societies of unequal civilization (Ch. III); peace and war (Ch. IV); the juridical organization of international society (Ch. V); and the individual conscience and international morality (Ch. VI).

[7] Taparelli even considers it essential to a well-constituted society that "the weaker States should be grouped into special confederations in order to balance the power of the greater States" (*op. cit.*, No. 1398).

· 2 ·

RIGHTS AND DUTIES OF STATES

★★

I. FUNDAMENTAL RIGHTS AND DUTIES

i. *Preliminary Remarks*

29. The human family, having spread all over the earth and established itself under every climate, has been broken up into a large number of partial societies, all of which have their own particular features and characteristics. This division, which was brought about by the very needs of occupation and human settlement, is a natural phenomenon and corresponds to the evident designs of God's providence.

In order to obtain for their members the general conditions needed for a truly human life, these groups were naturally led to organize themselves into States, and the latter, having their own specific end, which is distinct from that of the individuals which compose them, are true moral persons, endowed with all the rights which the fulfilment of their mission requires both in regard to their own subjects and to other societies of the same kind. These rights imply in turn corresponding duties towards the other States.

30. But the rights of a State are no more absolute than those of an individual. Their exercise is limited by the duty of respecting the equal rights of other States and of

submitting to the requirements of international collaboration.

31. The fundamental rights and duties of States were not created by the will of man. They are derived from the very nature and purpose of States, and are therefore natural rights and duties. All that custom and international agreements can do is to specify their import and determine their mode of application.

ii. *The Right to Existence*

32. A State consists of a territory, a population and a government. Every historically constituted State, as long as it can maintain sufficient peace and order within its territory and shows itself capable of fulfilling its international obligations, has a right to exist and to remain in existence. The other States are bound to respect it and to accept it as a member of international society.

33. A great variety of historical circumstances has brought about the rise of modern States, which have been formed by secession, dislocation or fusion. There is nothing immutable in the present political firmament, and new changes may take place in a more or less distant future. Furthermore, the origin of modern States has not always been above reproach, and many have been created in disregard of the indisputable rights of a pre-existing State. In such a case the latter can quite rightly defend the *status quo ante*. Other States have the right and may even have the duty of assisting it in such a task; but on no account are they to help dissidents or unjust aggressors. When it is not clear, however, on which side justice is to be found, or when the injured State, being incapable of defending its rights, has given up the struggle, a legitimate prescription may condone the irregular origin of the new State From that time onwards, it definitely acquires

the right to recognition by the other members of international society.

34. The right to existence which all States possess does not depend on the numerical importance of their population or the extent of their territory. It has been held in the past that the existence of small States was incompatible with the present-day needs of international life and constituted an intolerable anachronism. Experience as well as law has disproved this cynical opinion. Especially today, in a troubled world where right and might are too often at variance, the existence of small States which subsist only by the force of right is an eloquent tribute to morality and international justice. Being devoid of territorial ambitions and anxious for order and justice, the small States take the side of right most easily and almost instinctively in all the great international controversies. More than once the impressive unanimity of the small nations has sufficed to contain within the limits of justice certain imperialistic appetites about to be unloosed.[1]

35. The "right of national self-determination" has often been invoked in order to justify every separatist effort of

[1] Pope Pius XII, in his Christmas Message, 1941, showed clearly how the existence of small States can be safeguarded without disregarding the needs of political and economic life today. He wrote: "Within a new order founded on moral principles, there is no room for attacks against the freedom, the integrity and the security of other nations, whatever the extent of their territory or their capacity for defence. It may be inevitable that the larger States, with their greater resources and power, should aim at the constitution of economic groups in which smaller and weaker nations would be linked to them. But the latter, nonetheless, have an incontestable right (within the limits imposed upon them, as upon all, by the general interest of mankind) to the respect of their political liberty, the effective maintenance of their neutrality in international conflicts, in accordance with natural law and the law of nations, and the protection of their own development; for that is the only way in which they can adequately attain the common good, the material and spiritual well-being of their people."

57

national minorities which aspire to independence or wish to form a State with other groups of the same race. But this principle does not possess the absolute value which its supporters claim for it.

A national minority has undoubtedly the right to subsist within the greater collectivity whilst retaining and developing its own cultural characteristics. The State on which it depends must help it in this task to the fullest extent. But if, under pretext of safeguarding its unity, the State oppresses the minority by a policy of assimilation and uniformity, it is betraying its trust, and the separatist activity of the oppressed nation may be justified, as long as there is no other means of redress and the international common good is safeguarded.

If, on the other hand, the authorities do not arbitrarily identify the State and nationality, and, confining themselves to their task of security and general assistance, leave the racial groups under their care freely to exercise their cultural mission within the State, the secessionist claims of the minority are quite groundless.

But in no case can the mere advantage which a minority would find in becoming an independent political body or in uniting itself to another national State ever justify the unilateral severance of the bonds which unite it to a rightly organized political society. For usually the other members of this society have adapted themselves to a collaboration from which all have benefited and to which all have sacrificed something. Thus a close bond of solidarity has been created between all the members of this community, and no one has the right to reject it, lest grave damage be caused to its associates.

36. Recourse has also been made, in order to justify territorial readjustments or to oppose them, to the "theory of equilibrium" or "balance of power," which considers

that the best guarantee of international order against the unjust attempts of armed force is to be found in a well-proportioned arrangement of territories and other elements of political power (armaments, colonies, natural resources). For it is clear from history that a State strong enough to bid defiance to all its neighbours is inclined to abuse of this superiority in order to impose its yoke.

The argument of equilibrium could therefore be validly opposed to powers which were preparing to extend their territories unduly, to reinforce their armaments to a considerable extent or to make alliances which would have allowed them to disturb international policy. The objection seems all the more admissible as the States to which it is opposed have often used it themselves in the course of history against rivals whose political, military or territorial expansion they feared. But it would be wrong to give it an actual juridical basis and to consider equilibrium as a natural need of international life. In a well-ordered society of States, the right of a member should earn the respect of all the other associates by its moral force alone.

It is hardly necessary to add that the "balance of power" does not allow a State to seek at the expense of a third power the advantage taken from it by a fortunate rival.

iii. *The Right of Self-Preservation and Defence*

37. The right of existence implies for each State the right to take all the measures of self-preservation and defence necessary to safeguard its physical and moral integrity which are compatible with respect for the equal right of the other members of international society— namely, internal police, armaments, alliances, and even, in certain circumstances, intervention in the affairs of a neighbouring State.

As we shall study later on the problems to which the

right of intervention gives rise, we shall concern ourselves here only with the question of armaments and alliances.

38. The best way of ensuring that right will ever prevail over might is to reinforce the purely moral authority of the right with an equipment of material force. As long as international forces are not in existence to serve the community of nations, it is necessary to recognize the right of each State to raise and maintain military forces, to fortify its territory, and to manufacture arms and munitions in order to defend effectively its existence and its lawful interests against any aggression. On the contrary, it has no right to arm itself for the sake of ensuring that its ambitions shall overthrow the rights of others. Yet, how difficult it is, in practice, to determine the exact point at which armament ceases to be purely defensive and begins to serve aggressive aims! All States claim that they harbour no design of making war. But an all-pervading mistrust prevents these peaceful protestations from being believed; and every country takes the military superiority of its neighbour as the pretext for strengthening its own means of defence. Thus is begun, pursued and embittered that "armaments race" which the popes have denounced as the inevitable cause of incessant conflicts.

There is only one way of cutting short this Rake's Progress, for which each State, with more or less good faith, disclaims responsibility. It is to proceed, by means of an international convention, to the simultaneous and reciprocal limitation of armaments.[2] The well-intentioned

[2] This was the method recommended by Benedict XV in his message to the belligerents on August 1, 1917: "First of all, the fundamental point must be that the moral force of right shall be substituted for the material force of arms; thence must follow a just agreement of all for the simultaneous and reciprocal diminution of armaments, in accordance with rules and guarantees to be established hereafter, in a measure sufficient and necessary for the maintenance of public order in each State; next, as a substitute for armies, the institution of arbitration, with

efforts of the League of Nations to attain that end are known; no less notorious is the tenacious distrust that is the rock upon which that noble enterprise has hitherto been wrecked. Neither the institution of arbitration nor the limitation of armaments by international convention will, however, bring about the relief to which the Pontiff hopes these measures will lead, as long as all the States of the world, especially those which command the greatest war potential, do not sincerely and loyally adhere to the fundamental principles of international sociability and morality.

As long as no accord has been reached in this matter, no State will fail to base its argument for the maintenance or increase of its armaments upon its undeniable right to provide by its own resources for its own safety. It is a sound argument; but the only States which can legitimately use it are those which are prepared to collaborate, without hesitation or reservation, in the organization of arbitration, collective security and disarmament. In this, at the present time, lies the most compelling duty of all members of international society; and all Christian publicists should devote their endeavours to propagate the idea of arbitration.

39. By alliances, smaller States are given the possibility of adding to their military strength all the resources of the friendly powers with which they unite. They are allowable only if they proceed from a reasonable concern for defence. But, as in the case of armaments, it is very difficult to make an exact distinction between defensive and offensive alliances, and the desire to secure a balance

---

its high peace-making function, subject to regulations to be agreed on and sanctions to be determined against the State which should refuse either to submit international questions to arbitration or to accept its decision."

of the various political systems will inevitably bring into being a maze of alliances and counter-alliances as dangerous to world peace as the armaments race. So long as there is no collective organization of international security, individual States can make up for the insufficiency of their means of defence only by alliances; they can therefore quite rightly have recourse to them, in spite of the danger mentioned above. But this does not in any way lessen their obligation to help sincerely and without reserve in the building up of a more perfect juridical organization of international relations, which will secure for the right of even the smallest State the collective guarantee of all the powers.

40. Does the right of other third powers constitute an insuperable barrier to the right of self-defence possessed by every State? The opinion of the theorists of international law is very much divided on this grave question. For some, the need of self-preservation takes precedence over every other consideration: *Salus populi suprema lex esto* (Let the safety of the people be the supreme law). Others refuse to admit any alleged "right of necessity." They base their uncompromising attitude on the sacred and inviolable character of right, and insist on the flagrant contradiction involved in the recognition of a "right against right" in favour of a State in difficulties.

In this form the problem seems to be wrongly stated. It is not a question of determining whether the *fact* of necessity must prevail over a well-established *right,* but whether the right to existence which a State undoubtedly possesses must prevail over the equal right or a right of lesser importance possessed by a third State; it is a case of right against right.[3] Thus the conflict is one in appearance

[3] In connection with such a dispute, Taparelli remarks "It is precisely because of the apparent equality of rights that arbitration is necessary.

only, since right cannot recognize at the same time the contradictory demands of the parties involved. If the validity of one is admitted, the other cannot claim a hearing.

In reality the problem is more theoretical than practical, since the exception arising out of necessity can be admitted only under two conditions:

First of all, the necessity invoked must be real, extreme, and threatening the very existence of a State—to be or not to be. The danger of defeat followed by an amputation of territory does not constitute a necessity in the sense of which we are speaking.

Secondly, the State invoking necessity must not have brought about by its own fault the dangerous situation in which it finds itself. Thus an unjust aggressor could not plead necessity in order to make others bear the consequences of his crime.

It is hardly necessary to add that there are few cases in history when these two conditions have been present. But in the event of such a case arising, it will be sufficient to consult the general principles of morality and right in order to solve a conflict arising out of the case of necessity.

The rights of a State are no more absolute than those of an individual; they are limited by the respect due to the legitimate interests of other States and the needs of the common good of international society.

The right to existence is the first and most pressing right of a State; but it cannot prevail against the equal right to existence of another State which has remained a stranger to the circumstances that have caused the necessity.

The parties are obliged, in order to find a solution of their quarrel, to have recourse to impartial judges who can give an equitable decision" (*Saggio*, No. 1337).

But, on the other hand, this right to existence can rightly take precedence over a lesser right which another State could put forward. When a certain power, under stress of necessity, is led to disregard the right put forward by a neighbouring State, it is only compelling the latter to fulfil its obligations under the law of justice; in the case of a conflict of rights, the lesser right must disappear before the higher one.

iv. *The Right to Independence (External Sovereignty)*

41. The common good, which is the purpose of all social life, supposes the existence of an authority whose task it is to direct to this collective end all the particular activities of the associates. The right of determining in the last resort the rules to which all must submit their action, and of issuing orders which may not be disobeyed, belongs to the State and constitutes sovereignty.

The notion of sovereignty implies that the authority possessing it has a double right: that of effectively ruling the activity of the members of the social body and of rejecting any interference of other States in the exercise of its mission.

It is customary to speak of internal and external sovereignty. While taking into account the double aspect, positive and negative, of these complementary rights, it is more exact to speak of the sovereignty which the State exercises over its own territory and subjects, and of its independence in regard to other States. We shall now deal with the right to independence, the right of sovereignty being treated in section v of this chapter.

42. For various reasons some States find themselves habitually incapable of directing the activity of their subjects to the common good, and are obliged to demand or accept the advice and help of a foreign power in order to

fulfil their mission. They then cease to be sovereign and independent States and become protected States. When a government is incapable of securing the well-being of its subjects, a protectorate is quite a legitimate institution, as long as it is sincerely exercised for the good of the peoples thus placed under the tutelage of another nation.

43. There is nothing absolute in the sovereignty and independence of States. The measure and the limits of these attributes are to be found, first, in the actual requirements of the common good which it is the function of each State to provide for its subjects; next, in respect for the equal rights of other States and the obligation which is incumbent upon them all to promote the general welfare of the international community. So long as a State confines the exercise of its authority within these limits, it is entitled, on the ground of its independence, to refuse to allow any foreign interference either in its internal or its external policies.

44. Nonetheless, the history of international relations is very largely a tissue of continual interventions, in the ordinary sense of the word, which States claim the right to undertake in one another's internal affairs and foreign policies—interventions which may be armed or diplomatic, open or disguised, individual or collective.

One cannot pass a uniform judgment on all these interventions, and they must be considered on their merits. Often they have been resorted to by States which were ambitious and anxious to dominate; sometimes they appear to be a natural reaction against the abuse by a State of its right of sovereignty.

Intervention does not necessarily mean war. It can take all sorts of forms: diplomatic remonstrances, economic reprisals, embargo, peaceful blockade, military or naval demonstrations. War is the most extreme form of intervention, and can be resorted to only when other methods have failed, and for a very grave motive.[4]

In the absence of an international organization which is juridically organized and capable of keeping order among States, intervention will be justified in the four following cases:

(a) When a State has recourse to it to defend its legitimate interests which have been unjustly attacked or threatened by the internal or external policy of another power. In this case intervention is only the legitimate exercise of the right of self-preservation.

(b) When its object is to assist a third power, victim of an unjust aggression.

(c) When its purpose is to secure the respect of certain rules of the law of nations, the observance of which is of vital interest to all the members of international society.

(d) When it is undertaken in order to defend the rights of God, the rights of human personality and the overriding interests of humanity against barbarism and tyranny.

In the two last cases, since the object is to compel respect for juridical or moral principles of universal application, it is preferable that intervention should be effected by, or on the authority of, the organized community of nations.

45. In all these cases intervention is to be considered as the exercise of an undeniable right. There are many circumstances in which it may be strictly required as an obligation of international justice or charity. It is a duty

[4] See in Chapter IV the severe conditions which govern recourse to war.

of strict justice, when a State has bound itself by a treaty to assist another friendly or allied power in its lawful requirements. It is a duty of charity in all other circumstances, because the existence of a natural society of States imposes the obligation of mutual assistance upon each and all of them. But charity alone cannot oblige one State to incur heavy sacrifices and grave dangers in the interests of another power; for the purpose of the State's existence is, first and foremost, to protect the rights and interests of its own members. It would be false to this essential purpose were it to involve its subjects against their will in an adventure likely to damage their own more evident interests. Without doubt, the principle of solidarity can make it a duty for a nation to make sacrifices on behalf of the general welfare; but it does not require it to immolate its own interests for the benefit of a particular member of the international community.

Indeed it is preferable, in the interest of international peace and order, that such interventions should be as rare as possible. In the absence of an international authority qualified to determine what is right, there is always a great danger that States will be found to make the right of intervention an easy pretext for serving its own ends.

46. The principle of non-intervention has sometimes been opposed to the right of intervention as defined above. When expressed as an absolute and unrestricted rule of conduct, this principle has been formally condemned by Pope Pius IX (*Syllabus*, Proposition 62).

But this condemnation does not forbid a State to oppose foreign intervention in its own affairs or those of others, if it considers that it is injurious to its legitimate interests.

Likewise, concern for the superior good of the international society can rightly suggest a non-intervention agreement between the other States, which may be too much divided among themselves in order to judge the conflict properly, so that the internal troubles of a nation may not become the cause of a general war.

47. The unjust aggression against which a State is entitled to defend itself need not necessarily take the form of an unprovoked military attack. Only too often in the course of history have governments, urged by ambitions of conquest which they do not avow, interfered unduly in the internal affairs of another State in order to carry out in its midst the policy of *divide et impera* ("divide and conquer"). Such action aims at overthrowing and destroying the social cohesion of the State which is the victim of it, and to weaken its means of resistance so as to reduce it to servitude without the use of force or with the minimum of military compulsion.

These insidious tactics assume the most varied forms at the present time—the intrigues of a "fifth column," disruptive propaganda, the struggle of factions or the "class war." All these processes aim insidiously at undermining patriotism and substituting, for the loyalty due to the legitimate authority of the State, blind adherence to an ideology of which the leaders of the aggressor State set themselves up to their own exclusive profit, as the sole authoritative exponents.

Against this modern method of aggressive imperialism every State has the right to defend its integrity and its independence. It may, in particular, proscribe all seditious and disruptive propaganda or it may outlaw any organizations or factions which pursue objects incompatible with the loyalty due to the State, especially if they take their orders from a foreign power.

The other States have an undeniable right to come to the aid of a nation which is the victim of machinations of this kind. This intervention on their part does not necessarily imply recourse to armed force; vigorous diplomatic, financial and economic support may often be sufficient to reinforce effectively the victim's own resistance. There are times when such active assistance may be required of other States as a strict duty. This is the case when it is clear that such action is the only sure way to fend off the danger which the success of the aggressor State would bring to the international community as a whole. For "the triumph of the oppressor may cause greater and more imminent dangers for all the neighbouring peoples. That is why the defence of the oppressed nation is not only an obligation of good will for the adjoining peoples; it is also for them a question of public safety and national interest." [5]

Except in the case when intervention becomes a positive duty, a State can, in the present unorganized condition of international society, deliberately refrain from taking part in the conflict between two or more nations and proclaim its neutrality. It must then conscientiously fulfil all the duties which this attitude implies, and avoid helping in any way the cause of one or other of the belligerents. We shall deal later on in detail with the rights and duties of neutrality.

v. *The Right of Sovereignty (Internal Sovereignty)*

48. The sovereign power of the State is exercised not only over its subjects, whose activities it co-ordinates for the common good, but also over the territory which it occupies, and which it must dispose to the same ends. Thus sovereignty has two aspects: territorial and personal.

1. TERRITORIAL SOVEREIGNTY

49. Territorial sovereignty gives the State the right to use with full freedom its own territory, according to the needs of the common good of the society which it gov-

[5] Taparelli: *op. cit.*, No. 1263.

erns. This right, which can be opposed to any interference of another State, is distinct from the right of property which individuals exercise quite legitimately over various parts of this territory. Nor must it be confused with the more exclusive rights which the State possesses over its public and private domain.

By reason of this sovereignty, the State alone has the power to make laws within its frontiers, to maintain order and to provide as well as possible for the interests committed to its care.

As in all other matters, these powers are not absolute; they are limited by the duty of respecting the rights of other nations and of co-operating with them for the common good of humanity.

50. The territorial sovereignty of the State is exercised over a triple domain:

(a) The land.

Naval roads, ports and rivers are included in the national territory.

The needs of international commerce, in the maintenance of which all nations are equally interested, have naturally brought about some modifications to the right which each State possesses over its naval roads and ports, both of them indispensable to sea traffic. For similar reasons, the rivers which flow through the territory of several States are considered as opened to all nations.

(b) The sea.

Modern international law regards the sea as *res communis,* not to be appropriated but left to the free use of ships sailing under any flag. There is, however, one important qualification to this general principle: each State exercises particular rights of policing, navigation and fishing in the waters adjoining its own coast. This is a right of servitude rather than of ownership (*dominium*); this faculty is conceded to a State only to the extent to which it is necessary to safeguard its legitimate interests. No State may base upon it the claim to obstruct the peaceful passage of foreign ships. Even in time of war the territorial waters of a neutral State remain open to the passage of the fleets of belligerents, but the latter are forbidden to commit acts of war in those waters.

The extent of territorial waters has generally been fixed by custom at three maritime miles (about 5½ kilometres). Some States have, however, extended the limits of the coastal waters over which they claim to exert control. Actually there is a tendency in the theory of this matter in favour of a more elastic rule. Thus the width of territorial waters would vary according to the nature of the various interests to be safeguarded, the rights of the coastal State covering a sea area wider or narrower according to the requirements of fishing, of the customs police or of the prohibition of warlike operations.

(c) The air.

It is obvious that one cannot deny to the State its right of police and supervision in the air above its domain. But as in the case of territorial seas, an attempt has been made to harmonize the undoubted rights of the States with the reasonable demands of air traffic. This adjustment can be effectively brought about only by international regulation.

51. The territorial sovereignty of a State naturally implies the inviolability and integrity of its soil and frontiers. But in fact, history teaches us that this integrity is by no

means absolute, and that in the course of centuries the political map of the various continents has undergone profound changes. These territorial readjustments have generally taken place in one of the three following ways: occupation, transfer or conquest.

By occupation, territories which were previously under no sovereignty or were controlled by the nominal sovereignty of a power incapable of fulfilling its mission, come under the dominion of a State. As there are practically no unoccupied lands nowadays, this title can hardly be invoked.

Transfer is an essentially peaceful means of acquiring territory; it may take place by gift, exchange, sale, legacy. It was much used in former times when princes, who often mistook sovereignty for property, determined the fate of their own territories at their convenience, but it is hardly compatible with the modern view which considers the soil as the common heritage of the nation. In recent times it has been resorted to, under the form of lease, for the sake of giving some appearance of lawfulness to annexations made to the detriment of States unable to defend themselves against great powers in need of expansion.

Annexation, or conquest, is the only practical means of acquiring territory left today. We shall see later to what extent it can be reconciled with the demands of international justice.

52. (a) Recently, in international discussions, the voluntary cession of territory has again found a place. According to the needs of the situation, either a simple rectification of frontiers or an equitable redistribution of colonial possessions has been envisaged.

Claims to the former, usually not extensive, aim at remedying defects in the tracing of a frontier on the ground that it does not adequately meet the requirements of strategic defence or economic necessities or the principle of nationality. For the sake of peace there will often be circumstances in which it is wise to concede such a claim; in that case the State benefiting from the transfer ought to make equitable compensation to the State losing the territory. Unfortunately, experience shows how repugnant it is to the majority of States to make a voluntary renunciation of the smallest fractions of their domain, especially if elements of divers nationalities live together in the contested territory.

A transfer of populations has sometimes been advocated as the surest way of resolving the thorny problem. That is always a sad and painful expedient imposed by the necessity of avoiding even greater evils, such as persecution, massacres or war. It is a measure which involves tragic sacrifices for the transplanted population; it should therefore be carried out only on a very limited scale and everything should be done to make it easy for the displaced persons to become acclimated to their new home.

(b) The other claim, which has wider implications, is based upon the "right to living space." Some States indeed stress the poverty or overpopulation of their land in order to agitate for the revision of their existing territorial and colonial status.

In itself this argument is not without validity. A nation whose dense population can barely subsist on soil which is too poor or too restricted in area; a nation which, because of racial opposition, finds itself blocked from spreading into other countries, may lawfully insist upon its inalienable right to life. International charity makes it a duty for other States to leave to such a nation the requisite space to expand.

(c) But only rarely does this situation really arise; and there are remedies for overpopulation which are less extreme and less dangerous for the peace of the world. For instance, freedom of access to foreign markets will usually give a State the means of making up for the lack, within its own territory, of the raw materials indispensable to its industries.

Emigration, unless frustrated by an over-restrictive policy, will permit a country to send abroad the numbers in excess of the population which it can feed at home. This solution often involves the denationalization of the subjects obliged to leave their native land. But a State ought not to consider itself harmed by that very natural consequence of emigration. Its former subjects will not forget, in their new homeland, the links which bind them to their country of origin; and that country will find in the expansion of its economic and spiritual powers ample compensation for the loss.

(d) Further, it must not be forgotten that the tropical regions, which the advocates of a redistribution of colonial possessions particularly have in mind, provide only extremely limited opportunities of absorbing the surplus population of countries of the white race, and indeed of their economic expansion, whatever the popular view of the matter. Again, the interests of the peoples subject to the rule of the colonial powers must not be disregarded; and it is only too clear that they are not always compatible with the religious, moral, social and economic consequences which, in most cases, a change of sovereignty would imply.

(e) In no case, moreover, may a State use the argument of its own right to life and living space to attack the independence and integrity of another State.[6]

2. PERSONAL SOVEREIGNTY

53. Personal sovereignty gives the State the right of ruling over the members of the social body, of defining their rights and duties and of directing their activity towards the common good of the collectivity. In the exercise of this sovereignty over its subjects, the State is answerable to none of the other States taken individually; the society of States alone could have the power to intervene for the protection of minorities or the rights of the human person in cases of oppression.

The State still exercises its sovereignty over its subjects when the latter are travelling, and reside or have a domicile abroad, with all due respect to the rights of territorial sovereignty which the foreign State possesses over its soil.

Private international law and the agreements connected with it are very useful for avoiding conflicts in these difficult matters and for harmonizing the action of rival sovereignties for the greater good of all.

3. EMIGRATION AND IMMIGRATION

54. The great problem of emigration and immigration is closely connected with both territorial and personal sovereignty.

Man cannot live outside the bounds of all society, but he is not chained to the land of his birth and to his family

---

[6] "One nation's will to live must never amount to sentence of death upon another" (Pius XII: Christmas Message, 1939).

stock to the extent of not being able to break these bonds and start afresh in another social organism. As the maker of his own destiny, he has the right to "go forth out of his country, and from his kindred, and out of his father's house" (Gen. 12: 1) and to seek under other climes and in foreign nations the means of realizing the end for which he was created.

Futhermore, civilization can spread itself among the various branches of the human family only by a continuous and reciprocal communication of material goods and spiritual values. And it is evident that these fruitful exchanges are not possible without a wide and easy circulation of people and things throughout the world.

No State can absolutely forbid this circulation by right of sovereignty. In order to safeguard the interests under its care, it may make certain conditions for the departure of emigrants and the entry of immigrants; but its policy in this matter must always conform itself to the higher needs of the common good of humanity.

55. The country of origin has the right to make the emigration of its subjects conditional on the previous fulfilment of certain social duties, such as military service and the payment of taxes. Even more drastic measures could be taken to prevent collective emigration on a scale that would be gravely harmful; for in this case the interests of the social body must naturally prevail over those of the individuals anxious to leave their country.

The country of origin can also exercise, in full agreement with the authorities of the country of destination, a certain tutelary supervision of its emigrants, in providing as far as possible for their material, moral and religious needs. But these motives can never justify systematic opposition to all movements of emigration.

56. A policy of rejection on the part of the State of

destination is generally just as reprehensible. The latter has no right to consider that its own subjects are to be the sole beneficiaries of the resources of its territory and to keep a jealous monopoly for them. Its restrictions upon emigration must be justified by a reasonable concern for its own self-preservation. It may make conditions for the admission of emigrants which will prevent the latter becoming dependent upon it or disturbing order and public security (health, education, morality, private means, and so forth).

57. Certain countries are particularly severe towards emigrants who, by reason of their low standard of life, are likely to compete seriously with native labour, or whose racial difference is so great that they cannot be assimilated. These motives, which an exaggerated nationalism tends to magnify, justify a closer limitation of entries and appropriate measures of protection.

The bitter competition between native and foreign labour, which all agree in deploring, would be notably reduced by a proper control of the employment and wage-rates of the workers.

The pretext of racial differences is a far more serious one. The differences between the various branches of the human family are so great that the fusion of races, though it always remains physiologically possible, is fraught with so many moral and social dangers that it is not in any way desirable. One cannot therefore condemn absolutely any measure designed to prevent a harmful fusion of races. But justice and charity demand that the people so affected should be allowed a proper field of expansion on those continents which nature itself seems to have prepared for them.

58. The State must endeavour to establish cordial and peaceful relations between those immigrants which it

accepts and its own nationals, and it has undoubtedly the right to prepare, gradually and without violence, for their complete assimilation. With this object in view, it may impose its nationality on the foreigners definitely settled on its territory, or at least on their children born there, and expect from them a sincere and undivided loyalty.[7]

59. The question of political emigration is related to the problems examined above; many recent events have given it a tragic importance at the present time.

A noble sense of humanity leads the majority of States to help political refugees or victims of civil or religious persecution by offering them asylum. It is evident that those who take advantage of this hospitality ought to respect the conditions of their admission to a country, and should not, without the express or tacit consent of the authorities who have welcomed them, carry on any activity against the country or the regime from which they have fled.

As long as only a small number of individuals is con-

---

[7] In his Message of Pentecost, 1941, Pope Pius XII has outlined the benefit to be derived from a wise policy of migration which can furnish families with the living space which they lack in their native land. "When families migrating from one spot to another, go elsewhere in search of a new homeland, emigration, as experience shows, attains its natural end. We mean the more favourable distribution of men upon the earth's surface, suitable to colonies of agricultural workers: that surface which God created and prepared for the use of all. If the two parties, those who agree to leave their native land and those who agree to admit the newcomers, remain anxious to eliminate as far as possible all obstacles to the birth and growth of real confidence between the countries of emigration and the countries of immigration, all those affected by such a transference of people and places will profit by the transaction: the families will receive a plot of ground which will be native land for them in the true sense of the word; the thickly inhabited countries will be relieved and their peoples will acquire new friends in foreign countries; and the States which receive the immigrants will acquire industrious citizens. Thus the nations which give and the States which receive will contribute to the increase of human well-being and the progress of human civilization."

cerned, this forced emigration is but a slight burden for the States which have accepted them—a burden which is not sufficient to justify their intervention in the internal affairs of the refugees' country of origin. It is another matter when religious, civil or racial persecution provokes a mass exodus of inhabitants, deprived, for the most part, of their means of subsistence; the lodging and maintenance of such a multitude sets almost insoluble problems for the charity of neighbouring countries. The State whose sectarian policy precipitates a panic migration of this kind commits a grave offence against the most elementary duties of humanity and of international solidarity; and its cruel behaviour rightly brings upon it the sanctions of the civilized world. In these circumstances it is the duty of the international authority to organize the protection of the refugees and to help them to make new homes in the most hospitable countries that can be found.

vi. *The Right to Equality*

60. The fundamental identity of their nature and end confers in principle on all States, regardless of their importance, the same essential rights which the fulfilment of their mission demands.

61. One must not conclude that this basic equality, which is a consequence of their similarity of nature and end, allows all States to claim absolute equality of treatment on every occasion. As in the case of individuals, the actual conditions of structure, life and cultural development create accidental differences between States which must be taken into account in the organization of international relations. It would be quite unjust to wish to apply an equal treatment to societies which in fact differ very much from one another in features and character.

62. Unequal treatment can therefore be justified:

79

(a) By the need of certain States, whose weakness demands the help of other nations.

(b) By special circumstances arising from neighbourly relations, common racial descent, particular promises of mutual aid and assistance.

(c) By the incapacity of a State to fulfil its international obligations or to protect efficaciously the lives and property of foreigners residing on its territory. (Capitulations.)

(d) By the risks which the excessive ambitions of a State would cause to the safety of its neighbours or to world peace. (Compulsory disarmament.)

63. Capitulations or compulsory disarmament must not be considered as determining for ever the international status of a nation. But the latter can claim perfect equality of rights only when it has previously dissipated the legitimate mistrust which caused those special measures to be applied.

64. Equality of right is one thing, actual equality is another. Just as the right to private property which every man possesses should not entail as a consequence the complete levelling of fortunes, so a State cannot avail itself of equality of rights to claim its share in the territories of which other States have secured the just possession in the course of their development.

vii. *The Right to Promote National Interests*

65. Since States have been entrusted with the mission of promoting to the utmost the prosperity of the society committed to their care, they quite rightly claim the right to work without hindrance for the accomplishment of this task.

The spiritual and moral progress of nations comes about

in an essentially peaceful manner. Here there is no monopoly, no jealous covetousness; the scientific, artistic or religious values which enrich a nation radiate beyond its frontiers, without any loss to it, for the greater good of humanity; *licet divisus detrimenta non novit.*

It is quite different in the case of material progress. Here the resources and possibilities are limited, and their exploitation cannot fail to bring about ardent competition between the nations, which must be restrained by the law of international justice and charity if more serious conflicts are to be avoided.

66. Pope Pius XI underlines in his encyclical *Quadragesimo Anno* "the twofold aspect, individual and social, of property, according to whether it serves particular interests or concerns the common good." In the same way a double aspect, national and international, may be observed in the right which a nation exercises over the riches and resources of its soil.[8]

A State would do violence to the order of Providence if it claimed the right to administer its national patrimony solely for its own convenience, without any regard to the higher interests of humanity, leaving its natural resources undeveloped or refusing to make them available to other peoples who have an urgent need of them.

67. Nor can one allow the policy of absolute self-sufficiency of a State which, having retired within itself

---

[8] We shall not be misinterpreting the thought of the Holy Father if we transpose this passage of the encyclical from the civil to the international order, by slightly altering certain words: "The right *of using the resources of their territory* has been given to *nations* by nature, or rather by the Creator Himself, both in order that *each one* may be able to provide for its needs *of self-preservation and the subsistence of its members,* and also that by means of it the goods which the Creator has destined for the whole human race may truly serve this purpose. Now, these ends cannot be secured, unless some definite and stable order is maintained."

81

and being content with its own resources, would refuse its contribution to the economic progress of humanity.

This selfish policy, far from promoting the interests of the country which practises it, deprives it of all the advantages which follow, for individuals as for nations, from the division of labour and the exchange of goods and services.

68. By its unequal distribution of capacities and resources among the nations, Providence has clearly shown its desire to bring about between States an active system of exchanges, which are equally profitable to all who take part in them.

The definite and well-regulated order which must preside over international commerce does not forbid a State to defend against over-zealous foreign competition the industries which are already established on its territory or which it rightly desires to set up. But it will endeavour to use moderately, and only to the extent demanded by real necessity, the weapons provided by the over-stocked arsenal of protectionism; for the close solidarity which the Creator has established between nations and the mutual assistance which it implies demand that the barriers which are placed to the free circulation of goods should be reduced to a minimum.

It may even happen that charity can oblige certain States, in helping a country in distress, to promote the disposal of excess products which gravely threaten the balance of its economic system.

69. A similar concern for international good will should also moderate the bitterness of the competition which is witnessed in the search for international markets and in their exploitation. International order and peace demand that these efforts, which are legitimate in themselves, should finally result in a just equilibrium of commercial

exchanges and in a fair division of markets between the competing nations.

Treaties of commerce, negotiated in a spirit of justice and equity, agreements between producers of various countries, a proper adjustment of the various commercial policies brought about by wide and comprehensive international agreements, will effectively contribute to bring about this desirable result.

70. Such an adjustment is possible only if all nations allow their economic policy to be guided by those fundamental truths which, according to Cardinal Pacelli,[9] constitute the "spiritual framework of a sound international economy." "First of all, there is the fundamental unity of the great human family, whom Christ has told that it has one Father, who is in heaven; all the members of the various nations have the duty to reflect generously on other nations the love they are bound to manifest towards their own country; it means also that every nation has the duty to respect the legitimate interests of other countries. Furthermore, all nations are bound to practise justice and charity towards one another; this means above all, for all the States taken collectively, the furtherance and service of the international common good, in the same way as the citizens and rulers of each one of them have to further and serve a more proximate and less extensive common good; at the same time, all nations must realize their interdependence, and adapt corresponding methods of collaboration to each aspect of their solidarity; so that if they must, generally speaking, reorganize their national economic systems, they shall not systematically concentrate on themselves behind more and more impassable eco-

[9] Since his elevation to the papacy, the former Secretary of State of Piux XI has on many occasions renewed these exhortations, notably in his Christmas Messages of 1940 and 1941 (See Appendix I).

nomic barriers, but shall rather bring into honour the strict virtues which His Holiness Pius XI recommends in his last encyclical" (Letter of June 28, 1932, to M. E. Duthoit, President of the "Social Weeks" of France, on the occasion of the Social Week held at Lille).

viii. *The Duties of States*

71. States have not merely rights with regard to one another; they also have duties. These duties are of two kinds: duties of justice and duties of charity. Duties of justice, according as they regulate the relations of States among themselves or direct the activity of a State towards the common good of international society, depend in their turn upon commutative justice or social justice.

We must likewise distinguish in international charity a double impulse, according as it moves a nation to will the good of each State taken separately or the common good of the collectivity of nations.

72. The essential rights we have attributed to every State imply, on the part of the rulers of the other States, a corresponding obligation to respect them strictly.

A State which fails to fulfil this obligation lays itself open to the legitimate reactions of the injured party; and, if it persists in its injustice, it may be brought back by international law or by force within the limits of right, under conditions and restrictions which shall be explained later.

73. It sometimes happens that injustice aided by force will prevail over right. Success in itself cannot legitimate such a victory; but prescription may at last validate the *fait accompli*. However well-founded their grievances may be, the needs of the common good will not allow States which have been the victims of an injustice to question perpetually the concessions they have been forced to

yield. The order and peace of the world cannot suffer continuous upheavals of the international situation. This necessary sacrifice will not prevent those States from seeking by peaceful means the redress of the wrongs they have suffered.

It follows that "historic rights" are quite groundless and cannot justify the aims of bellicose nationalism.

74. Justice alone is not enough to win for mankind the great blessing of peace. It is much more the fruit of charity. The universal law of charity is as binding upon nations as it is upon individuals; it requires all States to show a sincere good will both to other States and to the international community.[10]

75. This benevolence will be evidenced, in the normal course of international life, by the customary signs of mutual respect and friendship, by a cordial exchange of information and services, by an open-handed welcome to strangers, by generous assistance of the victims of a national disaster, and by various other manifestations.

In times of conflict, charity, far from losing its rights, must govern more than ever the attitude of the disputants. It will lead rulers and people to make praiseworthy efforts to understand the mind of the enemy and to recognize how far its grievances are well-founded, to seek honestly the means of satisfying it, whilst trying to lessen in a spirit of conciliation the harshness of the letter of the law which they oppose to its demands.

Even when it has made concessions to the utmost limit, charity will not always succeed in appeasing a State whose ambition or cupidity knows no bounds. To violence

---

[10] "Peace is the work of justice, but only in an indirect fashion, inasmuch as it is the function of justice to remove obstacles to mutual understanding. But peace is the direct achievement of charity, for by its very nature charity begets peace; indeed love has, in the fullest sense, the power to unite" (St. Thomas: *Summa Theol.*, II-II, 29, 3, *ad* 3).

which scorns every right one must finally oppose force in the service of justice. But even in a war which it was unable to prevent, charity will still remain active. In the words of St. Augustine, it can desire victory only "for the good of the vanquished, and to bring them back to justice." As far as possible it will limit the use of force to the extent needed for the triumph of right, and will always refuse to give way to a spirit of vengeance.

Once the unjust aggressor has been vanquished, it will impose moderate and merciful conditions, which alone can obtain, together with the restoration of right, the re-establishment of concord and harmony.[11]

76. History tells us that the law which governs the relationships between nations has been purified and perfected only by the gradual substitution of more rational and just rules for the empirical and imperfect ones long sanctioned by custom and tradition. It is unfortunately true that so far war has been the chief agent of this evolution; nearly always, the new law has been set up on the ruins of the old, which had been violently destroyed for not having known how to yield spontaneously to the needs of a constantly progressing social life.

A more active exercise of international charity would easily prevent many an unfortunate conflict from taking place, by moderating the intransigence of nations obstinately attached to outworn rights, and by leading them to make opportune and salutary concessions, even in the case of most genuine rights.

77. Nevertheless there are limits to international charity. Though it may in certain circumstances advise

11 "There can be no stable peace or lasting treaties, though made after long and difficult negotiations and duly signed, unless there be a return of mutual charity to appease hate and banish enmity" (Benedict XV: *Pacem Dei Munus*).

and even command governments to make certain sacrifices, it can never allow them to compromise the rights of the nation entrusted to their care and which it is their bounden duty to defend against any encroachment.

II. RIGHTS AND DUTIES DERIVED FROM POSITIVE INTERNATIONAL LAW

78. The fundamental rights and duties of States, which we have just summarized, flow from the very nature of man and the needs of social life for which he has been made. But in order that they may govern effectively the life and conduct of nations, they need to be made more explicit, to be completed and adapted to the varying conditions of time and place by the constant additions of custom and agreements.

79. In the international order as well as in the more restricted sphere of private law, custom is a rule of conduct which has the force of a command of justice and equity. The compulsory nature of custom distinguishes it from mere international usage, and raises it to the dignity of an unquestionable rule of law.

80. The existence of an international custom presupposes the consent of several States, who agree in allowing it binding force. Thus there will be universal customs which all States are bound to respect, and particular customs which concern only a continent or an even smaller group of States. But this custom does not create law; it merely expresses it, and it is therefore evident that the refusal of one or the other States to yield to custom does not in itself dispense from the observation of a customary rule which has been generally received.

For a long time custom alone governed the relationships between nations, gradually extending its sphere and adding to its content as civilization grew and international life developed. But it remained uncertain and subject to dispute as long as its precepts were not defined in precise legal terms. In the case of certain very important matters—commercial relations, status of foreigners, territorial administration—States soon felt the need of determining by written agreements the mutual rights and duties they allowed one another. Eventually the advantages of this method ensured its permanence, and contractual law has gradually replaced customary law, without entirely eliminating it.

81. As States truly possess juridical capacity, they can create legal relationships between themselves by mutual consent, and can modify and even annul them. The document in which they set down their agreement is called a *treaty* in the broad sense of the word. But custom usually restricts the use of the term to those more important diplomatic documents, the purpose of which is to settle naturally divergent interests: treaties of peace, commerce, and so on. It also terms them *pacts* and *general acts* when they are supposed to embody the common views of the signatories. Other terms, such as *covenant, agreement, understanding, protocol, codicil,* are commonly used to signify less important undertakings.

Treaties are said to be *bilateral* or *multilateral* according as they are arrived at between two or several States. The latter are sometimes left open to the accession of other States which agree to assume the same liabilities. In that case, if they have been signed by many States, they are considered as treaties having the force of law, in contrast with contractual treaties which only bind a few signatories.

82. Treaties are to States what contracts are to individuals. Therefore, as regards the conditions of validity and binding force, one can rightly apply to them, *mutatis*

mutandis, the same principles which govern in private law the agreements concluded between private persons.

83. The validity of a treaty is subject to the three following conditions: competence of the authority concluding the treaty, lawfulness of object, and freedom of consent.

84. The method followed nowadays by all modern States in the making of a treaty hardly allows for a plea of lack of proper authority on the part of the chief negotiator of the treaty. Long negotiations usually take place before the signature of the diplomatic document, and the treaty acquires binding force only when it is ratified by the authority which the internal public law of each country empowers for that purpose.

85. In this matter, a doubt can arise only if the treaty has been made by an usurper who has seized power in defiance of constitutional rules. Would such a treaty still continue to bind a State on its return to constitutional legality? Jurists agree in upholding the validity of the treaty if the usurping government had been recognized by the other powers.

This purely external criterion does not satisfy the moralists, who are more concerned with the real consent of the nation which the usurper claims to represent. They solve the problem affirmatively if the nation submitted to the usurpation without opposing any effective resistance; in the negative, if it never ceased to show, by stubborn resistance, that it did not accept the intruding power.

86. A treaty is valid only if its purpose is lawful. Furthermore, no treaty of alliance or friendship can force a State to co-operate in an unjust venture of its associate.

87. It is essential for the validity of a treaty that the consent of the contracting parties should not be vitiated by error, fraud or violence.

There is no need to discuss the first two faults, since the close discussion which takes place between the negotiators of the treaty, and the very searching and critical examination which it undergoes before ratification make any objection on the ground of error or fraud extremely unlikely.

88. Threats and violence can furnish a more plausible argument to a weak State which has had to surrender to an ultimatum, or to a vanquished State which has had to accept the conditions of the victor. But the objection is valid only in the case of unjust threats or violence. A State which is defending a just cause is entitled, in the absence of an organized international jurisdiction, to use force in order to compel its adversary to respect or to restore its well-founded rights. But on the other hand, if force has favoured the designs of an unjust aggressor, a treaty made under such conditions could not in itself validly bind the State compelled to sign it. But other motives, derived from the interests of its subjects and the common good of international society, may oblige a victim of unjust violence to fulfil the obligations it has been forced to accept.

89. Treaties must be carried out in good faith according to the letter and spirit of the provisions they contain. As regards the interpretation of their terms, disputes may arise which neither party can settle unilaterally. To avoid the conflicts which easily arise in such matters, the contracting parties often nominate beforehand the arbitrators who will be called upon if necessary to decide between them. In practice many States have agreed to have recourse to the jurisdiction of the International Court of Justice.

The extent to which security and the stability of international relations depend upon the faithful observance by

States of the agreements which they have signed has been driven home by the painful experience of recent years. The harmonious and peaceful development of international life is not possible without mutual confidence. To use an expression of Theodore Roosevelt, the word of a ruler must be of such unquestionable solidity that one can build upon it as upon an unshakeable foundation.[12]

90. The parties remain bound in regard to one another all the time the treaty lasts. The latter normally ends either by the fulfilment of the stipulated terms, or by the ending of the period for which it was made. If it was made for a very long period or does not contain any time-limit, it can, as a rule, be annulled or modified only by the common consent of the parties. But if the latter are not able to reach an agreement, can one allow one of them the right to denounce unilaterally the agreements which circumstances have rendered unworkable or too burdensome?

This right cannot be denied; but in order to avoid the disappearance of all stability from the juridical relations between States, its application can be tolerated only under strict conditions and in clearly defined circumstances.

The existence of States stretches far beyond the narrow limits assigned to the life of individuals, and may cover centuries. If we consider the extraordinary changeableness of human things, we shall realize the grave impru-

[12] "May that mistrust be conquered, which weighs so heavily upon international law and obstructs all genuine understanding. May there be a return to the principle which makes good faith the inviolate sister of justice, to that loyalty to the pledged word, which is indispensable both to the establishment of firm and cordial relations between peoples and even more to the co-existence of powerful nations and weaker nations" (Pius XII: Christmas Message, 1940).

dence of measuring the length of international agreements by them. In consequence, permanent treaties can reasonably be accepted only under reservation of the tacit clause *rebus sic stantibus*: an agreement is valid only as long as things remain as they were.

To allow this interpretation does not imply the acceptance of the theory of the "conditional value of treaties," according to which an agreement ceases to bind a State when the latter no longer derives any advantage from its fulfilment. This argument is quite unacceptable, and its admission into international law would soon ruin the value of treaties.

91. The unilateral denunciation of a treaty can be allowed only under a double condition:

(a) The state of affairs must have altered so much that if the State could have foreseen it when it made the contract, it would certainly have refused consent.

(b) Before having recourse to unilateral denunciation, the State wishing to be freed from its intolerable burden must have exhausted every means of fulfilling the letter of the treaty and of bringing about, in conformity with its spirit, the modification made necessary by the new circumstances.

It is only when the defendant refuses to discuss and persists in demanding the literal fulfilment of the treaty, that the plaintiff can free himself from his obligations by a unilateral act of will.

92. It follows from what has just been said that no State has the right to cling obstinately to the letter of a treaty which events have rendered unworkable or excessively burdensome to the other party. Extreme justice approximates to extreme injustice, and the true spirit of

every treaty demands that the contracting parties should share equitably the advantages and the burdens.[13]

[13] For a long time international law provided no means of making these necessary readjustments. The authors of the Covenant of the League of Nations were well inspired when they decided that "the Assembly may, from time to time, advise the reconsideration by Members of the League of treaties which have become inapplicable" (Art. 19). Unfortunately, this Article was never applied. The Charter of the United Nations does not reproduce it, but makes some provision for the same need by authorizing the Assembly (Article 11, 3) to draw the attention of the Security Council to "situations which seem likely to endanger international peace and security." Article 34 also gives the Security Council "the right to investigate any dispute or any situation which might lead to international friction or give rise to dispute, in order to determine whether the continuance of the dispute or situation is likely to endanger the maintenance of international peace and security." Finally, under Article 35, "Any member of the United Nations may bring any dispute or any situation of the nature referred to in Article 34 to the attention of the Security Council or of the General Assembly." It must be remembered, however, that the abuse of this provision by members, far from contributing to the pacification of international life, may engender the most irritating insecurity.

3

RELATIONS BETWEEN UNEQUALLY
DEVELOPED POLITICAL SOCIETIES

★★

I. THE PROBLEM

93. The end of the political groups which divide the human family is to procure for their members the "full good of human life" (see No. 8). They approximate to this ideal aim, which their effort will never fully achieve, in very unequal degrees. Certain States have attained, at an early stage of their existence, a high level of material development and moral culture. Others have not gone very far in the process of civilization. And there are some nations which seem incapable of escaping by their own means from the bonds of ignorance and savagery. On the other hand, civilization is not the monopoly of a small number of privileged nations; all are invited to partake in its benefits, and the more advanced societies are bound to help the backward nations to lift themselves up gradually to a level of existence more in conformity to the designs of Providence. International solidarity finds its most fruitful form of application in this kind of assistance.

94. This educative influence cannot be exercised without a more or less close subordination of the assisted nation to the State which has undertaken to attempt its improvement. It may take the form of a freely accepted

guardianship exercised by means of advice, suggestions and persuasion, which respects to a very large extent the independence of the protected State. But this formula is rarely applied. Quite naturally the protecting State is led, in its efforts to fulfil its educational task, to substitute its authority for that which previously governed the territory it wishes to civilize. The assisted nation loses its status as an independent political society to become a protectorate or a colony.

This raises the very thorny problem of the legitimacy of colonization. Various titles have been invoked in order to justify it, and we must now try to determine their value.

II. GROUNDS ON WHICH COLONIZATION MAY BE JUSTIFIED

95. Let us first of all put aside the alleged need of an over-industrialized State for assured sources of raw materials and easily accessible markets for its goods. A wise and farsighted economic policy would always lead it to adjust its productive capacities to its normal resources and to the possibilities of sale on which it can reasonably rely; if it has been lacking in moderation and prudence, it alone must bear the responsibility, and it has no right to rectify its mistakes at the expense of the rights and liberties of others.

The reason brought forward has no foundation in fact. Many States which do not possess colonies are nevertheless gifted with prosperous industries and a flourishing trade; the extensive intercourse they maintain with other nations ensures for them an abundant supply of raw materials and numerous facilities for export.

96. Neither is the overpopulation of a State a more solid argument, as we have shown above (see No. 52).

97. Colonial conquest may take place, on the grounds
of first occupation, in territories occupied by savage clans
or tribes whose social relationships are anarchical, and
thus present an insuperable obstacle to civilization. In this
case—which is a very rare one—there is no dispossession
of a pre-established sovereignty. Authority, which constitutes organized society, does not exist; by enforcing its
own, the colonizing power acts as a first occupier, and
acquires without usurpation the undoubted right to rule
the territory it submits to its domination.

98. A civilized State can rightly dismiss from office a
native sovereign who has provided it with a grave and
just cause for intervention, such as attacks against the life
and goods of his subjects, breaking of solemn promises,
constant infringement of common frontiers. This is only
a natural application of the right of conquest, which we
shall deal with later.

To assert the theoretical validity of this title does not
imply the justification of all the conquests which have
taken place by the force of arms. Impartial history is
bound to declare that many colonial wars have been mere
acts of brigandage, devoid of any rightful title.

99. In modern times the colonial powers have shown
their preference for a title which seems to take more account of the rights of the peoples of the colonial territories
—namely, that of contractual cession. By treaties of friendship, alliance or protection, they obtain from native rulers
their voluntary renunciation of their rights as sovereigns.
There is nothing wrong in the principle of this procedure;
but the validity of these contracts is very doubtful in view
of the concrete circumstances in which they have been
brought about. In some cases, indeed, the circumstances
of the treaty offer very unsatisfactory guarantees both of
the validity of the powers possessed and of the full con-

sent given by ignorant and uncivilized chiefs who have concluded it. Recently, however, a number of treaties made between European powers and indigenous princes or chiefs have established a system of protectorate, which respects the authority of the latter and at the same time provides their country with an effective guarantee against external aggression and brings it the moral and material advantages of a more advanced civilization.

100. All the titles discussed so far are valid only in very special circumstances, and cannot serve to justify any sort of colonial expedition. Therefore, attempts have been made to discover titles of more universal application, capable of justifying in all circumstances the subjection of backward peoples.

This has led theorists to put forward the idea of the providential destination of the world's resources, and of the civilizing mission of colonization.

101. The Creator, who has shared out the riches of this world between the various parts and peoples of the globe, has nevertheless given them for the use of all men. The plan of Divine Providence must be respected, and the various human groups have no right to consider themselves as the sole beneficiaries of the wealth and advantages of the territory they occupy. Thence it follows that an harmonious and fruitful division of labour must be established between the nations in order to place at the disposal of all the members of the human community the resources of each part of the world.

The divine plan is distorted and humanity frustrated of its due when backward nations, through incapacity, slackness or laziness, fail to develop the potentialities of their territory. As long as there is no authority whose task it is to remedy this disorder, any State, provided it has the means and the will, may undertake this mission and can ·

97

withdraw if necessary from the native sovereignty the rights which it has proved itself incapable of exercising for the common advantage of all nations.

102. God has united men by close bonds of solidarity and made each one responsible for the fate of his fellow creatures: *Unicuique mandavit de proximo suo.* In national societies the education of the uncouth and ignorant masses comes from above and is the work of an elite. The same law governs the members of international society. The savage and degraded peoples, which are victims of vice, ignorance and superstition, nearly always need to receive stimulus, help, and guidance from an external source (that is, from a more civilized country) in order to lift themselves out of barbarity. Here again, in the absence of a properly organized international authority to whom this civilizing task would normally pertain, any nation which is willing and capable has the right, and sometimes even the duty, to take under its protection a still untutored population and to lead it as far as it can in the ways of progress and civilization.

103. It is argued against every justification of colonization, that as long as a true society of nations has not been organized, humanity remains divided into equal and independent societies, none of which has the right to exercise over the others any sort of jurisdiction or control. This objection is quite groundless. If a duly organized international society really existed, its task would doubtless be to ensure, either directly or indirectly, the development of the common patrimony of humanity for the good of all men and to exercise a beneficent tutelage over the still backward nations. These functions are necessary to the good order and progress of human society; and, in the absence of an international society capable of fulfilling them,

they pertain by rightful occupation to the first State which can and wills to exercise them.

104. In order that its work may not be incomplete and more harmful than useful, the colonizing State must not content itself with procuring for those under its care the material advantages of a higher culture; it must also give them, together with the higher blessings of mind and heart, the treasures of revealed religion. A purely material civilization, far from lifting up the soul of a nation, enslaves and paralyzes it and stifles the powerful natural instinct which makes it aspire to a higher ideal.

105. History is unfortunately a witness to the fact that, in the past as in the present, less disinterested motives have inspired the action of civilized nations. And when we remember the atrocities and pillages which have marred the beginnings of practically all colonial ventures, we may begin to doubt the value of an institution open to such terrible abuses.

Nevertheless an objective study of the actual results must lead one to a less pessimistic conclusion. In spite of the faults and crimes which have spoilt their beginnings, colonial ventures have on the whole given the subjected peoples more benefits than evils. They have abolished cannibalism, slavery, human sacrifices, the tyranny of barbarous potentates; a relative affluence has replaced the abject misery which starved the body and degraded the soul. It is true that one generation has had to pay for the establishment of foreign protection by excessive sacrifices; but a long posterity will benefit by the new regime it has brought about.

III. RIGHTS AND DUTIES OF THE COLONIZING POWER

106. Once the colonizing State has been rightfully invested with sovereign authority over the nation it has

99

undertaken to civilize, it exercises the plenitude of power in the territory it has taken over. It will use its power wisely and prudently in order to abolish practices contrary to the natural law, to purify customs and morals, to teach the habit of civilizing work, to provoke the rational development of natural resources, to ensure the defence of the country and to administer justice.

107. All these activities, which are performed chiefly for the good of the subject peoples, entail sacrifices on the part of the State which undertakes them, and they are compensated by the rational exploitation of the territories it controls. According to the plans of Divine Providence, international co-operation must benefit equally all the parties concerned. The colonial powers are therefore perfectly justified in demanding that colonization should pay its way and should remunerate their efforts.

108. A nation which has devoted its wealth and manpower to the humanitarian work of colonization has the right to demand in its turn, when necessity arises, the help of the natives to defend the parent-state. When answering this call, the colonial subjects are simply defending, as is their duty, the patrimony of material and cultural civilization which they share with those who have protected and educated them.

The serious objections to the use of native troops on the territory of the parent-state must force one to consider it as an extreme measure, to which recourse should not be had except in cases of very pressing necessity.

109. According to the fine maxim "Rule for Service," the rights justly claimed by the colonial authority are given to it only for the well-being of the population under its care. The interests of the latter must never be sacrificed to those of the parent-state; one must not allow the natives to be dispossessed of their land for the sake of

settlers, or permit a disguised serfdom to replace officially abolished slavery under pretence of educative work.

110. The education of the natives must take place gradually. It should imply neither systematic assimilation nor absolute conservation of ancestral customs. All that is good and respectable in the latter should be retained, and a wise temporization should preside over the elimination of abuses. Above all, one should be careful to attenuate the dangerous crisis which nearly always arises, to the harm of the less advanced races, when two unequal civilizations meet.

111. In order to achieve strong and lasting results, the colonial authority must, as far as possible, associate the natives with the task of civilization, and make use of their natural leaders, whose prerogatives have been maintained, as useful and influential collaborators.

112. All civilizing efforts will be fruitless if they are confined simply to the material order and neglect the moral and spiritual betterment of the natives. The colonizing State must add a fruitful religious activity to its economic work. It is obvious that it cannot itself actively engage in this apostolate; but it is bound to help to the fullest extent the official organisms delegated by the Church for this purpose.

113. The United Nations Charter formulates in Article 73 the duty of States which assume responsibility for the administration of territories whose populations are not yet capable of self-government. These States "recognize the principle that the interests of the inhabitants of these territories are paramount, and accept as a sacred trust the obligation to promote to the utmost, within the system of international peace and security established by the present Charter, the well-being of the inhabitants of these territories, and, to this end:

(a) To ensure, with due respect for the culture of the peoples concerned, their political, economic, social and educational advancement, their just treatment, and their protection against abuses;

(b) To develop self-government, to take due account of the political aspirations of the peoples, and to assist them in the progressive development of their free political institutions, according to the particular circumstances of each territory and its peoples and their varying stages of advancement;

(c) To further international peace and security;

(d) To promote constructive measures of development, to encourage research, and to cooperate with one another and, when and where appropriate, with specialized international bodies with a view to the practical achievement of the social, economic and scientific purposes set forth in this Article."

A high regard for the rights and interests of the colonial peoples is certainly the inspiration of these words. But the absence of any mention of the religious and moral interests of the native peoples and of the beneficent activity of the Christian missions unfortunately gives these lines an exclusively humanitarian flavour.

IV. THE INTANGIBILITY OF THE COLONIAL DOMAIN

114. As long as it conscientiously fulfils its tutelary mission, the State has an incontrovertible right to the peaceful possession of the colonial domain it has created. This right can be challenged only for one of the three following reasons: abuse of power by the colonizing State, incapacity to assume its responsibilities, transfer imposed as a sanction following a war unjustly provoked.

115. In the two first cases, the deprivation of a colonial

power in favour of a State which is more capable or better disposed is justified by the same reasons which make it lawful, in case of manifest incompetence, to dispossess the original native rulers of their title to sovereignty. But the opinion of one State alone is not sufficient to convict a colonial power of unworthiness or ineptitude for its task. Deprivation of sovereignty should be the consequence of a collective judgment. If the United Nations organization proves that it can function satisfactorily, it will be its business to pronounce that verdict and to designate the nation which is to take the place of the deprived State in the administration of the colony.

116. As for the colonial transfers imposed on a vanquished unjust aggressor, they take place on the same grounds and under the same conditions as the annexation of home territories by the victor of a just war.

It is obvious that in this matter the well-being of the native races must be especially taken into consideration.

117. The sharing-out of Africa which took place during the nineteenth century seems to have closed the era of colonial acquisition, as there are no more territories left for peaceful annexation.

Certain nations which have been comparatively late in expanding, and have few or no colonial possessions, are now demanding a redistribution of colonies in order to establish a just balance between States of fairly equal standing.

This demand cannot be based on any claim of strict justice (see Nos. 52(a) and 64). The latter does not require an equal distribution of goods and resources between States any more than between individuals. Otherwise it would also be possible to claim periodical revision of colonial holdings, in order to adjust them to the ever-changing equilibrium of civilized States.

The question raised by the revisionists is only a matter for international good will. The latter demands that nations abundantly provided with colonial possessions should allow free access in them to the labour and capital of less fortunate States, and should place the resources they obtain from them at the disposal of all. It can even, for the sake of peace, suggest to them to make certain liberal concessions to States which lack a proper field for expansion.

118. In these proceedings for revision, the plaintiffs tend to consider colonies as possessions which civilized States can dispose of or sell, grant or exchange at their own mutual convenience. International ethics cannot accept this over-materialistic point of view. It is more concerned with the native societies than with territories. It considers the education of the former to be a sacred work and a very delicate task which demands patience, sympathy, and especially continuity. Results which have caused much difficulty to obtain will be upset by the changes of method, legislation and regime which a substitution of sovereignty implies. This point is extremely important, and must not be forgotten in discussions of a possible distribution of colonial possessions.

V. THE EMANCIPATION OF COLONIES

119. Once a colonized nation, thanks to the protection it has enjoyed, has become capable of self-government, it naturally desires to be freed from subjection and to gain full independence. Thus a conflict arises between the colony demanding emancipation and the parent-state which is reluctant to grant it. It can be solved only by taking into account the equally respectable rights and interests of both parties.

120. Colonization means civilization, and civilization

means emancipation. Under pain of betraying its mission, the colonial power must listen to the rightful demands of its colonial subjects who have attained a higher level of individual and communal life, and must associate them to an ever-increasing extent with the government of the country. Like education, colonization must aim at becoming superfluous. As soon as its efforts are successful, it will be changed into a protectorate; and the protectorate will one day make way for a cordial and lasting collaboration between two free and equal nations.

121. Once emancipation has been achieved, the former colony must not break all the bonds which united it to the parent-state. A very real association has arisen between the two nations, which one of the parties must not repudiate at will to the detriment of the other, thus frustrating it of the just reward of its long effort.

This partnership, which must be the final aim of the relationships between the parent-state and the emancipated colony, preserves for the former the legitimate advantages it is entitled to demand from a land which has been rendered fruitful by the life and labours of its loyal sons, and ensures for the latter the permanence of those beneficent influences to which its betterment is due. If faithfully practised, it will benefit equally the interests of both parties and will become the rule of their mutual relations.

Secession would be justified only if, by reason of profound changes in the international balance of power, loyalty to the union would entail sacrifices to one of the parties out of proportion with the benefits derived by the other.

⋆4⋆

PEACE AND WAR

★★

I. INTERNATIONAL ORDER AND DISORDER

122. Peace, according to Saint Augustine, "is a good so great, that even in this earthly and mortal life there is no word we hear with so much pleasure, nothing we desire with such zest, or find to be more thoroughly gratifying."[1] It is nothing else but the tranquil security of an order of justice and charity which procures for each State, together with the full enjoyment of its rights, the most efficacious means of fulfilling its social mission and of contributing its share to the common good of international society.

123. It is evident that peace is the normal state of humanity, since it corresponds at once to the most pressing demands of human nature and to the law of Christ our Saviour, who Himself became our peace.[2]

Yet by a strange and distressing contradiction, the life of humanity seems to have been governed more by the rule of war than by the rule of peace. Paganism has not hesitated to give in all its mythologies a place to the god of war. The spread of the gospel law of love has not succeeded in pacifying or disarming men.

[1] *De Civitate Dei,* Book XIX, Ch. xv.
[2] "Ipse enim est pax nostra" (Eph. 11:14).

106

The reason for this is that justice and charity do not hold undisputed sway over the affairs of this world, but have to contend with the cupidity and ambitions of nations and their rulers which are powerful and active agents of conflicts and discord. And it often happens that the shortsighted judgment of man does not succeed in disengaging the sane and impartial solutions of justice and right from the confused conflict of pretexts and excuses invoked by the contending parties.

Harmony is disturbed, and disorder replaces order once a State's peaceful exercise of its right is disputed by another. This initial disorder is increased when the contending parties, having failed to solve their dispute by other means, resort to arms in order to settle their quarrel.

In former times the comparative isolation of States made it fairly easy to localize disputes and to prevent them from involving other States. Things are quite different today, and the close solidarity which unites all the members of international society implicates them, whether they will it or not, in any dispute which may arise in any part of the world.

124. The great precariousness of peace today imposes therefore on all governments the grave and sacred obligation of doing everything in their power to retain for the world the priceless benefit of this "most beautiful gift of God." [3]

First of all they must try to prevent, by a constant and straightforward exercise of justice and charity, the beginnings of any conflict likely to disturb order and peace between nations. If their efforts are unavailing, the parties in dispute are strictly bound to exhaust all means of peaceful solution before having recourse to war.

[3] Benedict XV: *Pacem Dei Munus.*

War itself, though lawful in extreme cases, is subject to laws which no pretext can allow the belligerents to disobey.

II. THE PEACEFUL SOLUTION OF INTERNATIONAL CONFLICTS

125. One can rightly deplore the fact that ever-recurring disputes threaten at every moment peace and harmony between States; it would be foolish, however, to be surprised at it. Relationships between States should be governed by right; but right itself is not always self-evident to the limited reason of rulers and nations, which itself is often obscured by passion. Besides, the constant increase of international relationships cannot fail to multiply to an equal degree the possibilities of clashes and conflicts. But peace will not suffer if the contending parties are sincerely desirous of settling these disputes in accordance with the demands of charity and justice.

126. Once a dispute arises between two States, their first and most pressing duty will be to seek the solution which is demanded by right, and not by their interests or ambitions. This is a matter for reason and not for violence. Force can, in some cases, strengthen the demands of right; it can never find or create it.

Conciliatory proceedings must therefore take place between the contending States. The inventiveness of man has devised so many forms of conciliation that there can be no legitimate excuse for avoiding this duty.

127. Very often straightforward *negotiations* between the interested parties will suffice to bring out their mutual good faith, to clear away misunderstandings and to simplify the complex elements which obscured the rule of right to which both parties profess submission. To achieve such a desirable result, it is very important that a

real spirit of good will and understanding should inspire the transactions between the negotiators. These requirements are not fulfilled when one of the parties to the dispute starts the discussion with the firm intention of refusing to listen to the case advanced by the other party and the determination to dictate its own conditions unilaterally.

128. It happens, however, only too often that the parties, obstinately clinging to their respective points of view, fail to reach an agreement. In this case the activity of an international authority, juridically constituted and having sufficient competence, could be usefully exercised in order to solve difficulties. In its absence, the disinterested and impartial intervention of a third power could help to bring about an harmonious conciliation between the parties. Every State has the right, and sometimes even the duty, to offer its *mediation* to the contending parties, as long as it possesses the necessary authority. The mediator must intervene between the two adversaries and suggest the terms of an equitable settlement, which takes into account at the same time their legitimate interests and the claims of justice. Sometimes, if the conflict has become a violent one, the mediator may, in order to hasten the restoration of peace, strengthen its good work by a military demonstration. This is called *armed mediation* and is perfectly legitimate when it is not destined (as, unfortunately, has too often been the case) to forward the selfish ends of the intervening third party.

129. The duty of the mediator is to propose the terms of compromise; it cannot impose them; the parties in question alone have the right to make a final decision. The latter, however, will often feel it difficult to accept the conciliatory solution suggested to them. Compromise always means the abandonment of some original claims,

and either side is loath to make any concession which would look like surrender. Their self-esteem is better safeguarded by an arbitral or judicial sentence which determines impartially the demands of right to which no one is ashamed to give way.

Arbitral awards are pronounced by an organism freely constituted by an agreement between the parties concerned; *judicial decisions,* by a tribunal which is permanent and therefore not likely to be influenced in any way by the litigants. Arbitral awards and judicial decisions, when they are freely administered and honestly accepted by the contending parties, constitute the best means of settling international disputes in a peaceful manner.

130. International law distinguishes between juridical conflicts and political conflicts. This distinction has a certain practical value, but it is difficult to justify it in theory. Every dispute, whatever its object may be, can always be finally reduced to a question of law—either natural or positive.

In practice, those disputes which concern a rule of positive law are regarded as juridical conflicts. Non-juridical or political conflicts are those which can as yet be solved only by the application of the very general laws which reason deduces from the primordial needs of human nature.

It is always possible to question, with more or less good faith, the validity of these deductions and, consequently, the binding force of the rules formulated in accordance with them. For this reason it has been a long-standing practice never to impose these rules on the contending parties by means of a judicial or arbitral sentence; it was thought that political conflicts could be solved only by the more supple methods of conciliation. Only juridical conflicts properly so-called, bearing on a question of positive law (interpretation of a treaty or a point of international law) or on the verification of some actual reality (materiality of the fact complained of, nature and extent of damage caused), could be submitted to an arbitral or judicial sentence.

Nowadays this distinction is tending to disappear, and there is an increasing tendency to consider conciliation and arbitral and judicial settlements as two successive steps of the same peace-making procedure which are applicable to all international disputes without exception, whatever their nature or object may be.

131. Progress in this direction is still impeded by notions difficult to eradicate. In the absence of an organized international society, superior to individual States and exercising a real power of jurisdiction over them, it is argued that a nation cannot give over to others the care and defence of certain essential values—for example, its honour, dignity, or vital interests.

It has therefore happened that until recent times these matters have remained the exclusive province of the States concerned and have been removed from any arbitral or judicial competency.

This is purely a matter of prejudice, and happily seems to be disappearing.

The honour of a nation, its dignity, or even its vital interests, can never be incompatible with respect for the rights of others. When a dispute arises about the requirements of the law, private citizens agree to submit their differences to the judgment of an impartial tribunal. It is difficult to see how the sovereignty and independence of States cannot allow them, in similar circumstances, to submit their quarrel to arbitrators or judges freely chosen by them. It is quite possible to constitute international courts of arbitration or justice which offer every guarantee of fairness and impartiality.

In the absence of this peaceful procedure, what remains to the contending parties except recourse to war? Who will dare to maintain that the latter will bring out and ensure the triumph of right more surely than the well-prepared and carefully grounded judgement of impartial and disinterested judges or arbitrators?

132. One objection still remains. In civil life there is a police force to enforce the decisions of the courts, but in the international order there does not yet exist any supra-national authority armed with sufficient coercive powers to enforce the submission of recalcitrant States to the judgement passed on them. This obvious gap will be filled up only by the foundation of a perfectly organized society of nations. But it does not excuse the nations from consulting arbitral or judicial organizations when disputes arise. These organizations will formulate the rule of law which they will have to accept. It is only when one of the parties refuses to accept the award that the other can have recourse to war.

133. Certain States claim the right to reject all proposals of arbitral or judicial procedure. The reason invoked is not valid. First of all, because it is very easy to fall into self-deception in these matters; secondly, because the common good of international society demands that no effort should be spared to settle disputes without useless shedding of blood.

134. Immediate recourse to the use of force is permissible only in three cases:

(a) When a State is forced to repel aggression suddenly initiated by an enemy;

(b) When a State goes to the aid of another State

which has been unjustly attacked and which it has promised to assist;

(c) When the adversary refuses to stop his military preparations and draws out negotiations only for the purpose of gaining time to increase his means of making war, and the organized community of nations refuses to intervene in order to prevent the imminent threat of war.

135. Since the end of the First World War there has been an intense and generous movement to bring into being a general system for the pacific settlement of disputes, to make it obligatory and thus to "outlaw war." It follows from the consideration set forth above, that it is the duty of States to give their full and loyal support to this pacific and humane endeavour.

III. WAR

i. *Its Nature and Lawfulness*

136. War [4] is an armed struggle in which equal and sovereign societies engage between themselves in order that what they consider to be their right or interest may prevail.

[4] It may seem surprising to find so much space devoted to war in this Code of international ethics. The reason is certainly not that Christian morality, like the pagan tradition, regards war as a normal institution of international life. War is a horrible evil and every effort must be made to prevent its outbreak. But it is not an absolute evil, and there are circumstances, though they be very rare, which justify a particular State or the organized community of States in having recourse to war. It is important to define these circumstances most rigorously. Further, if, in the solution of international disputes, war substitutes force for the regular processes of law, it is no less subject itself to the rule of law. It is the function of ethics to determine for the belligerents those rules of justice and charity which govern even the use of violence, and also to resolve, as far as possible, those problems of conscience— often acute problems—which the exigencies of modern war raise for individuals, citizens and soldiers.

It is *offensive* from the point of view of the State which begins hostilities; it is *defensive* from that of the State which has recourse to armed force in order to repel an attack. A war of *intervention* is one waged by a third party, a State which sides with a belligerent already engaged in battle and gives it armed help.

War must not be confused with certain acts of force used by States in difficult diplomatic negotiations in order to bring pressure to bear on the other party and to make it accept its demands more rapidly; for example, reprisals, seizures, temporary occupation of territory, peaceful blockade, embargo. The method is a dangerous one and runs the risk of developing into actual warfare; "peaceful restraint" is very often nothing else than an hypocritical euphemism to disguise a definite act of war, especially when it is exercised by a powerful State.

137. By the evils it inflicts on the territories on which it is waged, the confusions it brings about in international relations, the setback it inevitably causes to morality and civilization, war is always a terrible calamity and therefore cannot be considered as the normal means of settling disputes between nations. It should not find place in a perfectly organized international society; in the absence of such organization, the peaceful methods we have discussed above must always be preferred. Nevertheless war may be lawful in certain extreme cases.

138. In a society of independent States which have not yet succeeded in placing a supranational authority over themselves, it is above all necessary that the order of right and justice should prevail in order to ensure peace, which is an indispensable condition of prosperity and an essential element of the common good. If this order is seriously threatened by the perverse will of one of the associates and peaceful methods are unable to maintain it, all that

the injured State can do is to take the protection of its rights, or the redress of the injury suffered, into its own hands. Thus reason justifies a defensive war by which a State endeavours to repel an unjust aggression, an offensive war by which it seeks the restitution of an essential right, and a war of intervention by which an allied or friendly power gives armed assistance to a belligerent in similar circumstances.

Even in a perfectly organized international society, recourse to arms must be considered as the ultimate means left to the international authority or the community of nations to overcome a State which obstinately disregards the law and disturbs international order.

139. The commandment of the Decalogue "Thou shalt not kill" and the gospel law which prescribes non-resistance to violence and the pardon of injuries, have been quoted to prove the unlawfulness of war. This objection is based on a wrong interpretation of this double commandment.

The commandment "Thou shalt not kill" does not deprive individuals of the right of legitimate self-defence against an unjust aggressor. Nor does it do so, a fortiori, in the case of societies. Nor does the evangelical command not to resist evil and to pardon enemies imply the absolute repudiation of every war. Charity may command us to acquiesce without murmuring to the personal wrongs we have suffered; it does not in any way dispense public authority from its very definite duty of defending the interests and rights of the community under its care from all unjust attacks. As for the pardon of injuries and the charity we must show even towards our enemies, they are quite compatible with the conditions of a just war.[5]

[5] "These precepts concerning patience," wrote St. Augustine, "ought to be always retained in the habitual discipline of the heart, and the

Scripture and tradition, far from pronouncing an absolute condemnation of war, contain many passages affirming the lawfulness of a recourse to violence, especially when it is the only way to secure respect for justice and right.

140. In the face of the unanimous testimony of Christian tradition, certain pacifists will agree that in the past war may have been lawful. But they pass an absolute condemnation on modern warfare in view of the present development of armament technique, its unprecedented destructive power, and the increased solidarity of nations, which causes the smallest local dispute to have worldwide repercussions.

Even when restricted to modern warfare, the intransigence of such pacifism is indefensible.

First of all, it is by no means certain that modern wars are more terrible than the conflicts of the past, which made no distinction between the battlefront and back areas, devastated huge territories, delivered the civilian population to the exactions and violence of a mercenary soldiery which often changed sides but ever remained grasping and unruly, and brought with them famine, plagues and other nameless horrors.

---

benevolence which prevents the recompensing of evil for evil must be always fully cherished in disposition. At the same time, many things must be done in correcting with a certain benevolent severity, even against their own wishes, men whose welfare rather than their wishes it is our duty to consult. . . . And on this principle, if the commonwealth observe the precepts of the Christian religion, even its wars themselves will not be carried on without the benevolent design that, after the resisting nations have been conquered, provision may be more easily made for enjoying in peace the mutual bond of piety and justice. For it is a good thing to be vanquished if thereby one loses the possibility of doing evil" (*Ep.* 138, *ad Marcellinum*). As St. Thomas Aquinas justly remarks, "To pardon injuries one has suffered oneself is an act of perfection if to pardon is useful to others; but to tolerate patiently injuries done to others is an act of imperfection and even a vice if it is possible to resist the aggressor" (*Summa Theol.*, II-II., 188, 3, *ad* 1).

It must, however, be admitted that the system of armed nations and technical progress have made modern combats more murderous than those of former times. This must be remembered when determining the lawfulness of recourse to arms, since it is allowed, as we shall see later, only when the advantage expected outweighs the inevitable evils which must result. It obliges the champions of right more urgently than ever to exhaust all peaceful means of settlement before taking up arms.

The more or less deadly effect of methods of warfare affects only the forms of war and not its essential nature, and is not sufficient in itself to alter its morality.

Furthermore, a refusal to allow right the assistance of force in any circumstances simply allows force to take precedence over right with impunity, and delivers up humanity to the far more serious disorder of moral violence.

141. The very legitimate condemnation of the inevitable horrors of war must not lead one to include in its reprobation all belligerents without distinction. Only those deserve it whose injustice has brought about the commencement of hostilities; it cannot affect those who use force in perfect conformity with the demands of justice.

142. Catholic theologians and moralists, whilst refusing to condemn war absolutely, are careful to lay down the precise conditions with which a war must comply in order to remain within the limits of justice. They have constantly and unanimously taught that for a war to be lawful, it must

(a) Have been declared by a legitimate authority;

(b) Have a just and grave cause, proportioned to the evils it brings about;

(c) Be undertaken only after all means of peace-

117

ful solution of the conflict have been exhausted without success;

(d) Have serious chances of success;

(e) Be carried out with a right intention.

It is also necessary that moderation should characterize the conducting of hostilities and should keep the demands of the victor within the limits of justice and charity.

The following paragraphs will be devoted to a detailed analysis of these conditions.

ii. *Legitimate Authority*

143. The purpose of war is to maintain or assert the right of the community against external aggression. In the absence of a juridically constituted international authority, only those whose duty it is to defend and promote the legitimate interests of the social body can declare it.[6]

144. Several modern constitutions reserve the right of declaring war to the body of national representatives alone. The latter, however, nearly always finds itself faced with a definite situation and with the results of previous diplomatic deals which leave it practically no freedom of decision. The responsibility for the war which it is thus compelled to declare must be shared by the first instigators of the trouble, and by the clumsy or unbending negotiators who were unable or unwilling to solve it peacefully.

iii. *Just Cause*

145. Christian ethics admits of war only as a form of force to be used in the service of the right. The defence

[6] "The natural order of mortal things, ordained for peace, demands that the authority for making war and inflicting punishments should rest with the ruler. In obeying warlike commands soldiers should have an eye to peace and the common good" (St. Augustine: *Contra Faustum,* Ch. lxxv).

of an essential right unjustly attacked is the sole cause which justifies defensive war; in the absence of a properly organized international police force, the vindication of an essential right, unjustly contested, may also make war lawful; finally, the support of a belligerent who himself has a just cause of war alone justifies a war of intervention. In each of these cases the object is not to disturb order by recourse to arms but, on the contrary, to restore order. "War is waged that peace may be won." [7]

The sovereign [8] must not use his powers except in the general interest of the community committed to his care; consequently, war must not be undertaken for private ends or in the interests of a class or of a party. Again, the sovereign has no right to constrain his subjects to sacrifice their life and property for reasons of purely personal or dynastic interest or prestige.

146. Since in an actual case the contradictory claims of two contending parties cannot be equally right, it follows that both belligerents cannot have at the same time a just cause for war. [9] War can therefore never be objectively just on both sides, though subjectively each of the parties may believe it possesses a just cause for war.

On the other hand, it may happen that war may be objectively unjust on both sides, neither belligerent having a just cause for war.

In doubtful cases, when it is not clear on which side right is to be found, the conflict should never be settled by force of arms; it should be dealt with by the peaceful methods of conciliation and arbitration.

147. A State which has violated an essential right of

[7] St. Augustine: *Epistle 189, ad Bonifacium,* VI.
[8] Meaning the effective head or government of the State, be it monarchy or republic.
[9] "It is the injustice of the enemy which forces the wise man to make just wars" (St. Augustine: *De Civ. Dei,* Bk. XIX, Ch. vii).

another State and refuses to furnish the just reparation which is demanded, has no right to defend itself against the other party which has exhausted in vain all peaceful methods and now resorts to arms in order to obtain justice.

148. Justice sometimes changes sides in the course of negotiations or hostilities. For example, this may happen when a State which has a good and just cause for war refuses all sincere and reasonable offers of reparation. It can use force only to obtain satisfaction for the injustice it has suffered. Once this aim has been attained by the submission of the enemy, it cannot start or continue hostilities without being guilty in its turn of unjust aggression, and the State which it attacks can offer legitimate resistance.

149. It has been argued that it is useless to require the possession of a just cause to authorize war.[10] Without being quite so sceptical, one must admit that there exist some very intricate situations to which it would be difficult to give a safe and certain juridical interpretation. On the other hand, both rulers and ruled are prone to deceive themselves, under the influence of passion, as to the nature and extent of their rights. In the past these circumstances may have more or less excused the good faith of certain belligerents who had recourse to arms rather too readily. But nowadays, owing to the development of peaceful methods of conciliation and arbitration, we possess a very efficacious criterion for establishing the responsibility of the various parties concerned. At least the party which has rejected from the first all arbitral or judicial procedure which could have established clearly the de-

---

[10] "The ability to assign responsibility for aggression is always about the last thing to emerge, and belongs to the historian who studies and writes fifty years after a war and never to the politician who lives through the beginnings of a war" (J. Ramsay Macdonald, speech of September 4, 1924, to the Assembly of the League of Nations).

mands of right, and pretends to settle the conflict by
armed force alone, can never consider itself as authorized
to declare war.[11]

150. Other reasons apart from justice have been sought
to legitimize the use of force, such as common consent of
the belligerents, the need of the State, the prevention of
future aggression. These reasons have no foundation in
ethics, which considers that only the defence of an essential right can be a legitimate cause of war.

151. The need of the State, by which is generally
understood its interest or necessity, does not justify a war
which has been declared in violation of right. To allow
interest to take precedence over right would amount to
confusing expediency with justice, denying justice itself,
and shaking the very foundations of the order of human
societies. Nor is necessity a more valid excuse; a State can
invoke it only when that is equivalent to its right to existence and thus becomes a just cause of war.

152. There also exists a theory of "preventive war," according to which the State has a right to attack on preventive grounds another State which is still inoffensive and
peaceful, but which may be led at a future date, on
becoming aware of its increasing strength, to commit an
unjust aggression. The war which is thereupon declared
against it to ward off this danger is offensive from a military standpoint, but politically "defensive" and could thus
claim a legally just cause.

The doctrine is indefensible, since it would leave the
way open to arbitrariness and thus legitimize every kind
of abuse.

A preventive war against a possible aggressor is iniqui-

[11] Rightly enough Pope Pius XII denounced on September 14, 1939,
in speaking to the Belgian Ambassador to the Holy See, "the abandonment of this principle of negotiation" as the determining cause of the
catastrophe which had just befallen mankind.

tous of its very nature. A ruler who would claim to regulate his policy according to a still uncertain future could
allow himself every kind of surmise and would have no
difficulty in imagining a distant menace which would give
a plausible pretext to his ambitious or rapacious aims.
Peace and international order would soon disappear under
a regime which allowed recourse to "offensive-defensive"
war for the most imaginary grievances.

Only a very real and imminent menace—such as a
systematically aggressive policy, an unusual concentration
of troops, and the like—can authorize a State which considers that it is menaced thereby, to demand the cessa-
tion of these suspicious activities, and, in case of refusal,
to impose it by force.

iv. *A Grave and Proportionate Cause*

153. The justice of the cause for which a belligerent
takes up arms does not in itself suffice to legitimate his
decision. Right reason further demands that the importance of this cause should be proportioned to the gravity
of the evils which inevitably follow upon a war.

154. It may sometimes happen that, owing to the circumstances which accompany it, a quarrel may become
far graver than the trivial or unimportant incident which
brought it about. In that case, the State which persistently
refuses to grant the small reparation claimed greatly ag-
gravates its original fault. Likewise an injury sustained by
the ruler may, in consequence of an obstinate refusal to
make reparation, involve the honour of the whole nation
represented by its head.

In minor conflicts, which do not immediately involve
any of its vital interests, a nation will often find occasion
to practice that charity which the law imposes on societies
as well as on individuals. Secure in the self-evidence of its

rights, it will know how to temper with a largehearted tolerance the demands of absolute justice, and will thus open the way, more surely than by arms, for a sincere and lasting reconciliation.

v. *A Reasonable Hope of Success*

155. Even when there is a just cause of war, a State may not initiate or enter into a struggle which, from all the available evidence, will end in disaster and aggravate the injustice which it desires to rectify. In these conditions there is no advantage to be weighed in the balance against the sacrifice which a declaration of war would impose upon its subjects.

This consideration does not, however, invalidate the universally recognized right of a State unjustly attacked to oppose violence to the violence done to it. *Vim vi repellere omnia jura permittunt.* Besides, it is indeed rarely that the issue of a war can be predicted with certainty, however unequal the chances of the belligerents may appear to be. Divine Providence often confounds the most objective human calculations; interventions may suddenly arise which upset the initial balance of forces.

On the other hand, a higher obligation—that of respecting one's plighted word, of defending the higher values of religion and civilization, and so forth—may sometimes lead to choosing an heroic defeat instead of an inglorious capitulation. The nations which have been martyrs to their duty render a supreme testimony to right which echoes throughout the centuries and keeps humanity faithful to the cult of honour and justice.

vi. *Concern for the International Common Good*

156. In weighing the legitimate advantages he expects from war, and the various evils which inevitably follow

upon it, the just belligerent must take into account the heavy load of suffering and ruin which the conflict will impose upon other nations, both upon those whose military help he expects and upon the neutrals who will feel the painful repercussions of the struggle. This comparison will often reveal such a disproportion between the fruits of victory and the price which the whole of humanity has to pay, that it will be a duty of charity to forgo the just reparation rather than to expose the world to a dreadful catastrophe.

vii. *War, "the Ultimate Argument of Kings"*

157. "Only under compulsion and reluctantly should one come to the necessity of war," wrote Vittoria (*De jure belli,* 467, 60). War is an instrument which States are allowed to use, in certain circumstances, in order to enforce the respect of right on those who would wish to disregard it. But it is a terrible instrument which should be used only when all other means have failed. War will always remain the ultimate argument of kings; *ultima ratio regum.*[12]

viii. *A Right Intention*

158. As in every other human action, war, which is legitimate in itself, may be vitiated by the wrong intention of the one who wages it. This does not make a war objectively unjust; but a belligerent may compromise the righteousness of his cause because he is actuated by other motives, such as greed or cruelty or a spirit of revenge.[13]

---

[12] Henry of Ghent: *Quodlib.,* XV, q. XVI: "There are two ways of combatting: by discussion or by violence; the first being peculiar to man and the second to wild animals, one should have recourse to the latter only when the former is of no avail."

[13] St. Thomas (*Summa Theol.,* II-II, 40, I): "The intention of those who make war should be a right one—namely, that good should be pro-

159. This right intention, demanded by the moralists as an essential condition of a legitimate war, may easily agree with other motives which are more interested, but are still in conformity with right and reason.

IV. THE CONDUCT OF HOSTILITIES

i. *General Principles*

160. Even under the state of violence constituted by war, the moral law keeps all its rights, and its precepts continue to govern all the acts of the belligerents.

These precepts, in actual fact, can be summed up in a few rules of very wide application which need more positive definition if they are to govern effectively the conduct of war. In every age nations have attempted to do this. First of all custom, then later on pacts and bilateral treaties, and finally general conventions, have progressively worked out the set of rules codified by the law of nations under the title of "laws of war."

All belligerents are bound to conform their acts of war to these laws.[14] These rights have considerably helped to attenuate the original horrors of war, and any State which disregarded them would be guilty of a crime against humanity.

---

moted and evil avoided. Thus St. Augustine says that the true adorers of God regard those wars as peaceful which are not undertaken out of cupidity or cruelty, but are waged for the sake of peace, so that the wicked may be punished and the good assisted." And St. Thomas concludes that "even though the war has been declared by a competent authority and for a just cause, it may become unlawful by reason of the wrong intention of the one who wages it. For St. Augustine says that the desire to harm, the cruelty of vengeance, a warlike spirit, enemy to all peace, the fury of reprisals, the lust of domination, and similar things, must be condemned in war."

[14] "Even between enemies," wrote St. Ambrose, "certain rights and conventions must be respected" (*De Officiis*, Bk. I., Ch. 29).

ii. *The Declaration of War*

161. We have seen that war is allowed only against an unjust State which obstinately persists in its wrong-doing. Before any forcible action is taken against the disturber of right order, time should be given him to repent and to make reparation for the damage he has caused. The original incident should be made the subject of preliminary negotiations, proposals of conciliation and arbitration, and so forth. If all efforts to solve the dispute peacefully fail owing to the obstinacy of the culprit, a solemn warning should inform him that the hour of diplomatic negotiations is over and that he has now to face his responsibilities. Hostilities cannot commence "without a previous and unequivocal warning, which shall take the form either of a declaration of war, giving reasons, or of an ultimatum with a conditional declaration of war" (Second Hague Conference, 1907: *Convention Relative to the Commencement of Hostilities*). It goes without saying that, in order to safeguard the last remaining chances of peace, there should be a reasonable delay between the notification and commencement of hostilities.

iii. *Acts of War*

162. In answer to the question "What is permissible against enemies in a just war?" Vittoria replies: "In a just war, one has the right to do everything that is necessary for the defence of the public good" (*De jure belli,* No. 15). But according to the great teacher of Salamanca—as can be seen from the context—this right is limited by the demands of morality and natural law.

163. The needs of warfare will never allow belligerents to commit actions which are wrong in themselves, such as treason, the breaking of solemn oaths, assassination,

slanderous charges, and similar things. The end does not justify the means, and no advantage, however great, must be gained at the expense of a violation of the moral law.

164. Morality also forbids brutality and useless cruelty. No doubt, "war is war" and cannot be undertaken without destruction, bloodshed, and the loss of human life. The just belligerent can cause these inevitable evils to his adversary, but only to the extent needed to curb his wrongful obstinacy. To overstep these bounds would be a violation of justice and charity. In the choice of the methods of warfare and of lethal weapons, it is certainly permissible for a State to select those which, without exceeding the limits of natural morality and positive international law, will hasten the end of hostilities and reduce its evils.

165. Some have been sceptical enough to say that war, being essentially inhuman, cannot be made more humane. Others say that, on the whole, the most humane type of war is a relentless one which, by the terror it inspires, promptly breaks the enemy's resistance. All this is pure sophistry which Christian morality cannot countenance.

War is a struggle between men, not between wild beasts bent on mutual destruction; it is therefore something essentially human and subject to the laws of humanity. The just belligerent still considers his enemies as creatures made to the image of God—creatures who, in spite of their wrongs, are still entitled to his repect and love.

Since he is compelled to use force and violence against them, he will do so only to the extent required by the rightful cause he has undertaken to defend. These ethical requirements have been sanctioned by the positive law of nations. Article 22 of the regulations respecting the law and customs of war on land adopted at The Hague in

1907 expressly says that "the rights of belligerents to adopt means of injuring the enemy are not unlimited." This principle was unanimously adopted by all the States represented.

On the other hand, it is extremely doubtful whether the cruel and implacable severity of a belligerent would promptly disarm a terrorized enemy. On the contrary, experience has often shown that these barbarous methods, far from shortening the war, prolong the resistance of the exasperated enemy, provoke terrible reprisals, and transform the struggle into a blind and inhuman massacre.

166. The Church has always tried to humanize the methods of waging war because she considers that it is a human affair; others, who do not claim her patronage but are nevertheless inspired by her ideal of peace and charity, have tried to do the same; their united efforts have resulted in those "laws of war" which all civilized nations have accepted and which they are bound in conscience to respect.[15]

[15] Over and above the prohibitions contained in special agreements, the "Regulations Respecting the Laws and Customs of War on Land" (Hague Conference, 1899 and 1907) especially forbid:

(a) To employ poison or poisoned weapons;

(b) To kill or wound treacherously individuals belonging to the hostile nation or army;

(c) To kill or wound an enemy who, having laid down his arms, or having no longer means of defence, has surrendered at discretion;

(d) To declare that no quarter will be given;

(e) To employ arms, projectiles, or material calculated to cause unnecessary suffering;

(f) To make improper use of a flag of truce, of the national flag or of the military insignia and uniform of the enemy, as well as of the distinctive badges of the Geneva Convention;

(g) To destroy or seize the enemy's property, unless such destruction or seizure be imperatively demanded by the necessities of war;

(h) To declare abolished, suspended or inadmissible in a court of law the rights and actions of the nationals of the hostile party.

"It is likewise forbidden a belligerent to force the nationals of the hostile party to take part in the operations of war directed against their

167. (a) The alarming progress of science and technical knowledge constantly puts at the disposal of belligerents more and more powerful instruments of death and destruction—air and submarine warfare, chemical and bacteriological warfare. It would be futile to contest the right of States to adapt, to some extent, their armaments and methods of combat to these new possibilities; and on many points the development of military technique involves continuous revision of the laws of war.

(b) In the event of a belligerent breaking any one of the laws of war, is his enemy entitled to retaliate in kind? Great as may be the danger that such reprisals will cause the opposing sides to rival one another in savagery and ferocity, it seems difficult to deny this right to the victim of such a breach of the law, particularly if the reprisals are of such a nature as to oblige the enemy to return to a respect for legality. But it is never permissible to reply to acts of one's opponent which are intrinsically criminal by crimes of the same kind—for instance, to make reprisal for a massacre of entirely innocent people by putting other innocent people to death.

---

country, even if they were in its service before the commencement of the war" (Art. 23).

The five powers which took part in the Washington Conference, 1921–22 (the United States of America, the British Empire, France, Italy, Japan) spoke of "the use in war of asphyxiatory, poisonous, or other gases, and all analogous liquids, materials or devices" as justly condemned by the general opinion of the civilized world, declared their assent to their prohibition, and invited all other civilized nations to do the same. (Treaty of Feb. 6, 1922.)

In 1925 a protocol on broader lines, open to the signature of all nations, extended this prohibition to bacteriological methods of warfare. At the present time this protocol has been ratified by about thirty nations.

(c) The just belligerent may use against his enemy any means of constraint which is not itself intrinsically immoral, on condition that his employment of such measures does not constitute a useless net of cruelty.

It is a very laudable and humane consideration which has led States to accept the prohibition, by international convention, of certain particularly deadly weapons, of which it is difficult if not impossible to control and limit the destructive effects (for example, chemical and bacteriological warfare). It would be a great advance in the humanizing of war if the powers were also to agree to outlaw other armaments whose appalling capacity for destruction are already known. It is, of course, understood that all States are strictly bound to respect engagements which they have undertaken under this head. Since the last World War, the use of the atomic bomb looms large among the methods of warfare which are particularly objectionable; for its formidable power of destruction extends without discrimination to every element of the population, military or civilian, without the possibility of confining its appalling effects either in space or in time.

iv. *Prisoners of War*

168. It is chiefly by the treatment meted out to prisoners that wars between civilized nations differ from those between barbarians. Savages merely consider prisoners as defenceless enemies on whom they can revenge themselves with impunity, or whom they can reduce to slavery. The progress of civilization has generally improved the lot of prisoners, whose lives are now spared and who are granted means of subsistence, humane treat-

ment, and, when peace has been signed, are sent back to their homes.*

The older moralists show much less mercy to prisoners.[16] Nowadays, when armies are recruited by conscription, the combatants are rightly presumed not to be guilty, and the customs of modern warfare, which have been confirmed by the second Hague Conference (1907), explicitly forbid the execution of prisoners. It is therefore a ruling of positive law which belligerents are bound to obey in strict justice.

169. It is absolutely clear, therefore, that prisoners have a right to live. But it remains to be seen whether the just belligerent is obliged to accept the surrender of soldiers who lay down their arms, or can make a rule that no prisoners are to be taken.

The order to give no quarter, which is dictated by hatred or revenge, and turns the struggle into a ruthless massacre, is absolutely immoral. Some military regulations allow it "in cases of absolute necessity," but the second Hague Conference did not admit this exception and prohibits the "no quarter" order entirely.

* This is the general rule, codified in the existing customary law. But conventions made for the express purpose of protecting the human rights of prisoners cannot reasonably be invoked to compel repatriation, if prisoners are themselves convinced that they would suffer the loss of life or liberty if returned to their country of origin. In that event the principles governing the granting of asylum to refugees from persecution apply (see No. 59 above).—Ed.

[16] Francis de Vittoria held that "there is nothing to prevent prisoners or those who have surrendered from being put to death if they have been found guilty." It is true that the writer supposes that the prisoners have been found guilty, and his further remarks soften this doctrine considerably: "In war there are many customs established by the law of nations, and it is generally admitted in the habits and usages of war that, once victory has been gained and all danger averted, the prisoners should not be put to death, unless of course they have fled; in this connection the law of nations must be obeyed to the extent that men are accustomed to do so" (*De jure belli,* No. 49).

It may sometimes happen that the military authorities forbid their troops to accept gestures of surrender, on account of previous misuse by the other side. In that case, this measure, however severe it may be, can be considered as a means of legitimate self-defence which is justified by the bad faith of the enemy.

v. *The Treatment of Non-Combatants*

170. (a) If recourse to force is lawful only against those who unjustly impugn a right or who, having violated it, refuse to make reparation for the damage they have caused, it follows that the just belligerent cannot, on principle, use violence against those who have not in any way sided with injustice. On this point the Christian tradition is quite definite: *Numquam licet interficere innocentes*—"It is never permissible (deliberately) to kill innocent people."

(b) The application of atomic energy to warlike purposes poses a most delicate problem, and moralists are far from being united upon the solution of it.

Some think that the use of the atomic bomb should not be absolutely condemned, on the grounds that it is the quickest and most effective means of destroying the whole military and economic apparatus of the enemy and of convincing him that prolonged resistance is useless. The death of thousands of innocent people, they argue, is not desired as an end in itself but is simply tolerated as a concomitant effect inevitably associated with the principal end in view.

Others, on the contrary, considering the impossibility of limiting in space and time the ravages of the atom bomb, contend that the use of it should be prohibited for the same reason that the poisoning of wells or the systematic massacre of the enemy population is forbidden.

Yet other moralists allow for a distinction arising from the circumstances and the objectives of an attack by atomic weapons; for instance, it is one thing (they would say) to drop an atomic bomb on an enemy fleet in mid ocean, and quite another thing to drop it on a great industrial centre.

It must be remembered that we are dealing here with a new implement of war of which it is not yet possible to foresee the appalling range of destruction. One thing seems certain: it can never be right to use the atom bomb against elements of the population whose actual participation in a war is only very remote, with the intention of breaking the enemy's will to fight through the horror of the dreadful massacres which this deadly weapon causes. And all those who draw their inspiration from the Christian tradition will agree in hoping that the use of the atomic bomb will be outlawed by an international convention.[17]

Until such a convention has been concluded, and until there is sufficient assurance that it will be strictly observed by all the powers, it seems difficult to deny States the right to build up a stock of atomic weapons for purely defensive purposes. The fear of immediate reprisals would very probably induce a State to refrain from using these terrible implements of war, knowing that others possess them as well. It was thus that, during the Second World War, the belligerents abstained from using poison gas, because they knew that each side was equally equipped with it.

[17] Taparelli, anticipating in the middle of the nineteenth century our present means of destruction, wrote: "To poison the water, promote epidemics, to use infernal machines of too wide a radius of destruction or certain weapons which make excessively cruel wounds—all this is illicit and contrary to the law of nations" (Taparelli: *Saggio*, Book VI, Chapter I, par. 1354).

171. But though the belligerent cannot make any direct and intentional attempt on the lives of peaceful inhabitants who take no part in the war, he is not forbidden to do certain things in the course of the struggle which will necessarily bring about the loss of innocent lives. This loss is not directly willed as a means likely to break the resistance of the enemy; it is permitted or tolerated as a secondary effect which is inevitably bound up with the legitimate end in view.

For these reasons it is permissible to fire against centres of military resistance, even if by so doing there is a danger of hitting private houses, schools, hospitals, and causing the death of non-combatants. Likewise, unless there is a contractual agreement to the contrary, it is lawful to make use of bombing planes to attack munition factories and railway junctions situated far from the firing line, in spite of the inevitable loss of innocent lives brought about by these expeditions.

Nevertheless, there must be a reasonable proportion between the lawful end sought by the belligerent and the harm to innocent people which results from it against his direct will.

172. (a) The old moralists had no difficulty in establishing a very clear distinction between combatants and non-combatants. The mercenary armies were but loosely related to civil society in general and made war almost on their own. It is a very different matter in these days. Now, the whole nation identifies itself in some way with its army; business men, financiers, workmen, railwaymen, sailors, civil servants, all work night and day to equip and supply the armed forces. The patriotism of "the rear" sustains the endurance of "the front," and public opinion supports

the government and encourages it to persevere in its resistance to the enemy.

Thus war has become national and "total" war, and almost all the citizens, in divers capacities, take an active part in it. The distinction between combatants and non-combatants becomes more and more blurred and the civilian population has ceased to be "innocents" in the sense in which the moralists of an earlier age understood the term. Belligerents have the right to take account of this evolution; they certainly took advantage of it in the last two world wars. New methods of war have appeared and they must be judged by moral principles; among them are wholesale blockade, aerial bombardment of open towns, the use of the atom bomb, the taking of hostages, and the forcing of civilians to take part in activities which serve the military purposes of the enemy.

(b) The blockade of a besieged town has always been considered as a normal and legitimate means of breaking the resistance of the invested place. During recent wars this measure has been applied to the whole of enemy territory. General blockade is designed, in the intention of the belligerent enforcing it, to exert upon the civil population a gradual pressure which will end by inducing it to come to terms.

This is a formidable weapon; but it does not appear that the use of it ought to be prohibited, for it becomes deadly only through the obstinacy of the people blockaded when they prefer the most extreme privations to capitulation. But, as far as possible, the belligerent carrying out the blockade ought to moderate the rigour of it for the benefit of children, the aged and the sick, and of those innocent people whose territory is in the temporary occupation of the enemy.

(c) The laws and customs of war have long forbidden the bombardment of "open towns." Since they offered no resistance to occupation, to bombard them was clearly an act of useless cruelty of which the civilian population was the principal victim. Nowadays, however, bombardments do not serve only to prepare for the capture of an enemy's town; besides the so-called "bombardments of occupation," a far more important part is now played by "bombardments of destruction" aimed principally at damaging, dislocating and putting out of action everything in a city, township or village, which serves directly or indirectly the enemy's war effort. In our day, installations and services of this kind are dispersed all over the territory of a country and are the targets for the opposing belligerent's air attacks.

The classical distinction between "open town" and "fortified place" is consequently out-of-date. It can no longer be invoked to deny the just belligerent the right to launch massive and destructive air raids against any agglomeration which shelters the enemy's war factories, depots of arms and munitions, or the administrative, economic and financial services of his military machine.

The authorities who order these air raids are nonetheless bound to restrict their destructive effect, as far as they can, to objectives which directly or indirectly serve to sustain the enemy's resistance. It is wrong for them to proceed methodically to destroy a town, quarter by quarter (saturation bombing), or to scatter death haphazard in order to terrorize a peaceful and unarmed population. For the same reason there should be no hesitation in condemning air attacks carried out at so great an altitude that all accurate aiming becomes impossible, or in condemning the shooting into the stratosphere of flying bombs or rockets to which it has hitherto been found impossible to give a precise aim.

On the other hand, the power and mobility of antiaircraft defence have largely helped to transform vast territories into fortified zones, in regard to which the enemy's air force is not obliged to observe such limitations. Further, the extreme skill with which belligerents camouflage their military installations and their whole apparatus of war, often makes it difficult for their adversaries to keep the rules which prudence and humanity dictate.

(d) The military authorities of a power which invades or occupies enemy territory often seize hostages who are to answer with their lives for the security of the invading or occupying forces. This practice, derived from the customs of savages and designed to make the innocent pay for the guilty, is incompatible with the demands of morality. Hostages cannot justly be held responsible for assaults or disorders in which they have had no hand, and to put them to death for hostile acts committed by third parties is quite clearly a crime; and indeed a futile crime—for daring men who risk their lives in schemes directed against the enemy are unlikely to be deflected from their purpose by the prospect of the consequences which ensue for hostages.

It is equally criminal to place a curtain of inoffensive civilians in front of a force of assault troops or to place hostages on points or objectives which are particularly exposed to hostile attack, such as military buildings, war factories, railways or ships.

(e) A belligerent has no right to dispose arbitrarily of the freedom of the inhabitants of occupied territory. He is forbidden to force them to give him assistance in a way which involves their direct participation in his struggle against their own country—as, for instance, forced enrolment in his armed forces, economic collaboration or the giving of information.

The Second World War was distinguished by wholesale deportations in which peaceful citizens were torn from their homes, the sacred bonds of conjugal and family life were broken, whole populations were reduced to a state of virtual slavery and the victims of these odious slave raids committed to the most degrading promiscuity. The precepts of ethics and the positive rules of the law of nations alike condemn all such crimes.

173. In their anxiety to protect the lives of innocent people from unjust attacks on the enemy's part, the old moralists were much more easy-going concerning the treatment of the property of a peaceful population. Yet they insisted that only real necessity could justify the destruction of such property.[18]

In the modern laws of war an endeavour has been made, and not without success, to increase the protection of civilian property against arbitrary exactions. It is not always easy, however, to draw a clear distinction between those goods which serve and those which do not serve the

---

[18] Vittoria writes in his *De jure belli* that "it is certain one can take from innocent people goods and other things the enemy would make use of against us, such as arms, ships, engines of war. For otherwise, victory, which is the purpose of war, could not be attained. Furthermore, one can take away the money of the innocent people, and burn or destroy wheat, if that is necessary to weaken the enemy forces" (No. 39). But he adds immediately an important proviso: "If war can be carried on properly without despoiling the peasants and other innocent people, it seems that it is not permissible to despoil them" (No. 40).

purposes of war. In point of fact, all the enemy's resources, wherever they may be, can be used to prolong resistance, and the adversary should be permitted to take or even destroy them, if necessary, without regard to the rights of their lawful owners, by bombing, fires, requisitioning, and similar means.

Nevertheless, the laws and customs between civilized nations make it a duty for them to spare, as far as possible, those buildings which, by their very nature, cannot be put to military uses: churches, libraries, historical monuments, and the like.

174. Those things which the necessities of war permit in combat naturally cease to be lawful once the struggle is ended and the victor occupies, at least provisionally, the territory he has invaded. The regime of occupation has its laws which the just belligerent is bound to observe.

175. Until the nineteenth century, custom allowed that the mere fact of military occupation—*occupatio bellica* —gave the occupying power full sovereignty over the territory it had taken. It could therefore govern it as a true and final possession, impose its laws, raise taxes, and use both its people and its goods in the struggle against the former possessor.

This practice is inacceptable, since it implies that force alone can be a source of right.

A fairer principle is applied today. The territory remains *de jure* under the authority of the evicted sovereign, but, as he can no longer rule it, the occupying power takes his place in the very interests of the inhabitants and fulfils the functions of a legal government until the conclusion of peace, which will finally settle the fate of the occupied territory.[19]

[19] "Of themselves the acts of public administration of the occupying power have no validity, but the legitimate authority (of the legal govern-

176. The "Regulation Concerning the Laws and Customs of War on Land" which resulted from the deliberations of two Hague Conferences (1899 and 1907) has defined the rights and duties of the occupying authority and successfully reconciled the real necessities of war with the imprescriptible demands of justice and humanity.

The occupying power shall endeavour to restore and make secure both public order and life by respecting whenever possible the laws already in force in the country. The inhabitants are not to be forced to take part in warlike operations against their own country. The honour and rights of the family, the life of individuals, as well as religious beliefs and the practice of religion, must be respected. Private property cannot be confiscated. If the occupying power collects taxes instead of the legal government, it must use them for their normal purpose. If it raises other taxes, they can be used only for the needs of the army or the administration of the occupied territories. No collective fine shall be levied on the population by reason of individual acts for which it cannot be considered as jointly responsible. Requisitioning of goods and services can be demanded only when accompanied with a just indemnity.

177. The occupying power provisionally owns the possessions of the enemy State situated in the invaded territory. But on principle it is allowed only to administer them. Goods which can be made use of in military operations may nevertheless be taken by the occupying army, even if they belong to private individuals. Municipal property, and goods belonging to religious, charitable,

---

ment) tacitly ratifies those which are demanded by the general interest, and this ratification alone gives them juridical value" (Cardinal Mercier: Pastoral Letter, *Patriotisme et Endurance,* Christmas, 1914).

educational, artistic or scientific institutions, shall be treated in the same manner as private property.

178. (a) The inhabitants of the occupied territory retain their allegiance to the legal government of the country; they merely owe to the occupying power an external submission which does not affect their loyalty. They are not allowed to commit acts of individual or collective violence against the army or administration of the enemy; these acts, which are useless for their cause, inevitably provoke reprisals.

(b) The State which is the victim of unjust aggression and which has been obliged to abandon to the invading army the whole or a part of its territory, retains the right to organize secretly forces which, in response to its appeals, will support within the country the action of the armies of liberation.

In the absence of orders from the lawful authorities, the active resistance of the population under enemy occupation can still be justified as the exercise of their legitimate right of defence against any injuries of which the occupying power may be guilty in violation of the law of nations, such as deportation, forced labour for the enemy or compulsory service in his forces. Even so, the resistance must never assume an anarchic character; it must be carried out in a disciplined way and with due respect to the requirements of international morality.

V. The Re-establishment of Peace

179. "It is with the desire for peace that wars are waged," wrote St. Augustine (*De Civ. Dei*, Book XIX, Ch. xii). Peace, which, according to the same writer, is the "tranquillity of order," necessarily implies the restoration of justice and charity between nations. A truly just

and lasting peace is the supreme aim which morality assigns to victory.

In theory, it is the just belligerent who is entitled to victory. In actual fact, however, it often happens (by the permission of Divine Providence, whose inscrutable though merciful designs cannot always be fathomed by the limited understanding of men) that military success forsakes the cause of justice and crowns the wicked designs of a criminal State. We must therefore examine two hypotheses: the just belligerent overcomes his adversary, or is defeated by him.

i. *The Just Belligerent Is Victorious*

180. War is allowed only when it is the sole and necessary means of defending an essential right which is unjustly attacked, or, if that right has been violated, of obtaining adequate reparation. This purpose is attained as soon as the unjust aggressor gives up his attempts and sincerely offers to give full satisfaction. From that moment the victor gravely compromises his cause if he rejects these proposals and continues hostilities.

The principle is quite clear, but its application raises thorny problems which the mere application of the law of "rigid justice" does not suffice to settle.

181. First of all, what are the conditions which the just victor has a right to dictate to an enemy who surrenders unconditionally?

These conditions have been summed up by Suarez under four headings, which in modern times may be called *restitution, reparations, sanctions* and *guarantees.*

"Complete satisfaction comprises:

> 1. The restitution of all the goods unjustly detained by the adversary;

2. The reimbursement of expenses incurred owing to the injustice;

3. It is permitted to use certain sanctions by reason of the fault committed, for in war there is place for vindicative as well as commutative justice;

4. It is also permitted to demand all that is necessary for the conservation and defence of peace, since the chief purpose of war is to lay the foundations of a lasting peace" (*De tripl. virt. Theol.*, T. III, disp. XIII, sect. vii, no. 5).

These lucid and precise formulae do not call for any further comment.

182. In principle, reparations should cover all the expenses and damage which war has caused to the just victor. But this demand of "rigid justice" will often be seriously mitigated by considerations of advisability, the requirements of the common good, and especially the law of charity.

The disasters caused by the great wars of modern times are nearly always catastrophic in extent, and the transfer of sums owed in reparation raises almost insoluble technical problems. The wholesale removal of enormous sums of money causes economic perturbations which affect even those who benefit by them. Furthermore, charity does not allow one to require from a State, however culpable, more than it can normally pay.

There are two ways of avoiding this difficulty.

First of all, one may spread out the payment of the sums demanded over a great number of years, by adjusting the annuities to the capacity of the debtor State. This would satisfy both technical requirements and the demands of charity. But this method, by making the vanquished nation feel for too long the effects of defeat, tends to foster resentment and is hardly likely to bring about the re-establishment of a sincere and lasting peace.

The victor may also seek indemnification by finally taking possession of a portion of the enemy's territory. This raises the problem of annexation, which we shall deal with later.

In the letter *Quando nel principio,* which he wrote on June 24, 1923, to his Secretary of State, Cardinal Gasparri, His Holiness Pius XI showed how it was possible, in the thorny problem of reparations, to conciliate the demands of justice and those of charity:[20]

183. (a) All the theologians are at one in recognizing the right of the conqueror who has justice on his side, to punish the guilty men who unjustly caused the war.[21] But certain reservations must be made to the right which the just victor has to inflict public retribution.

[20] "When, with the intention of repairing the very important damages suffered by populations and districts formerly prosperous and flourishing, the debtor (that is, the State owing this reparation) gives proof of a serious determination to arrive at an equitable and final agreement, soliciting an impartial decision upon the limits of his own solvency and pledging himself to furnish the arbiters with every means of arriving at a true and exact estimate of his resources, then justice and social charity, as indeed the very interest of the creditors and of all the nations, exhausted by wars and athirst after tranquillity, seem to oppose the claiming from the debtor what he would be incapable of giving without draining himself entirely of his own resources and of his own capacity of production. For this would result in an irreparable injury to the debtor as well as to the creditors themselves and in the danger of social unheavals which would be the definite ruin of Europe, and of rancours which would keep up a continued menace of new and more disastrous conflagrations.

"Similarly, it is just that the creditors should possess guarantees proportionate to the amount that is owed to them and which assure the recovery of it, upon which depend interests vital to all."

[21] Vittoria considers this as a natural right, "seeing that otherwise society could not hold together unless there was somewhere a power and authority to deter wrongdoers and prevent them from injuring the good and innocent" (*De jure belli,* No. 19).

The fact that he acted in good faith may often be a valid excuse for a belligerent who (objectively) had no just cause to go to war; he does not deserve punishment for a sin of which he is not consciously guilty.[22]

Considerations relating to the common good will sometimes make it wiser for the just victor to mitigate his exercise of the right of vindicative justice, or even to forego it altogether.[23]

(b) In his Christmas Message in 1944, Pope Pius XII allows the necessity and the lawful character of vindicative justice and lays down the conditions of wise moderation which should govern the application of it.

"As for those who have taken advantage of the war to commit real and proved crimes against the law common to all peoples, crimes for which supposed military necessity may have afforded a pretext but could never offer an excuse—no one, certainly, will wish to disarm justice in their regard. But should it be claimed to judge and punish not only individuals but whole communities, all must see in such a procedure a violation of the code which governs every human tribunal."

(c) The sanctions applied in the name of vindicative justice must fall only upon those who are really guilty; they must not be inspired by hatred or revenge, as they would be, if the just conqueror endeavoured to penalize, without any regard to their

[22] "It sometimes happens (indeed, often) that not only the subjects, but even the rulers, who actually do not have a just cause, go to war in such good faith that they cannot be considered as guilty" (Vittoria: *De jure belli*, No. 59).
[23] "Reason demands that vindicative justice should be exercised to the least possible disadvantage of the common good" (Suarez: *De tripl. virt. Theol.*, sect. VIII, No. 3).

real responsibility for the guilt of the war, all the citizens of the defeated State.

(d) For a long while victors in war hardly thought of exercising the right of penal retribution which Christian morality allows to them. It was thought that the right of war, as a natural attribute of sovereignty, was not subject to moral judgment. Crimes and injustices committed in the course of hostilities were regarded as regrettable but inevitable incidents, of which both sides were equally guilty and over which the treaty of peace discreetly drew the veil of a general amnesty.

In modern times, wars are no longer localized, and the unspeakable sufferings which they inflict on the whole world have suddenly reawakened the conscience and moral sense of the peoples. These therefore summon the rulers responsible to answer for the evils which, by the reckless or unrighteous use of force, they have loosed upon mankind. On the other hand, in some armies contempt for the laws of war has been so erected into a system, that the excesses of the soldiery necessarily involve the responsibility of the military leaders and members of governments who have tolerated and approved them or even ordered them to be committed.

During the First World War a powerful movement of public opinion in the Entente countries insisted that these crimes against the law of nations and humanity should not remain unpunished; and it was in deference to these legitimate demands that the peace treaties of 1919 and 1920 required the punishment of the principal war criminals. The whole question, however, had not been sufficiently brought to a head and the sanctions provided in the treaties became a dead letter. Without contesting the claim of the victors to exercise vindicative justice, many people felt that such action was fraught with insuperable difficulties. Who was there to be sure of discovering the guilty? Who would appoint the judges and ensure their impartiality? What authority was there, able to confer competence and jurisdiction upon them? By what criterion would the courts measure guilt or innocence? And from what code were to be derived the penalties to be inflicted upon the prisoners found guilty? The final difficulty was to determine by what right one could punish acts which, at the time they were committed, were not forbidden by any written law.

(e) These scruples did not prevail over the horror provoked by the unprecedented atrocities perpetrated during the Second World War. Well before the end of hostilities the United Nations [24] declared their intention of punishing all war criminals without distinction of rank or status. For this purpose they drew up on August 8, 1945, the procedure which they proposed to apply. To each of the Allied States was given the power to entrust to its own courts the punishment of crimes committed in the war on its own territory. The guilty persons were to be judged and punished in conformity with the laws of that State. But the major war criminals, whose deeds had extended beyond the frontiers of a single state, were to be brought before an international military court. The Charter of August 8, 1945, determined the heads of the indictment under which the arrested men were to be tried: crimes against peace, crimes against the law of nations, and crimes against humanity. The

[24] The title here used refers to the wartime alliance, not the United Nations Organization.

rights of the defence were to be strictly respected. Against the prisoners found guilty the tribunal would pronounce sentence of death or inflict whatever other punishment fitted the gravity of the crime.

This kind of procedure, provided it be applied with absolute impartiality, is destined to fill a serious lacuna in modern international law. Hitherto, those responsible for a war had to answer for their acts merely to a remote posterity which could only too easily forget and forgive. In future they will be far more conscious of the heavy responsibility which they have assumed, since they know that they will have to face the judgment of their contemporaries and in due course suffer just retribution for their crimes.

Until such time as there is a universal acceptance of the moral principles which determine the rights and duties of the just victor in the repression of war crimes or until an international court, whose jurisdiction is universally recognized, has been set up, the action already taken by the United Nations in this matter certainly provides international morality with a valuable and effective sanction.

Of the three headings of accusations laid down by the Charter—crimes against peace, against the law of nations and against humanity—the first requires precise definition. Not every war is in itself criminal, not even an offensive war, if it be declared for the purpose of constraining a State which has violated another's rights and obstinately refuses to make the reparation which has rightly been demanded of it. It is only a war of aggression, undertaken with no lawful justification whatever, which should be considered a crime against the peace. Consequently it is very desirable that the real nature of this "crime against the peace" should be the subject of exact definition, incorporated in a convention to which States as a whole would subscribe.

(f) The provisions of the Charter of August 8, 1945, have not, however, disarmed all criticism. Indeed, many people are reluctant to approve a form of repressive justice which is enforced only against the vanquished and turns the blind eye to any crimes of which the victors may be guilty. They would have greater confidence in a court whose members were not at one and the same time judges and interested parties, but in which judges chosen from nations less directly interested in the case were on the bench.

It must be admitted that the unilateral character of the repression of war crimes, which is that of the Charter in question, does not give full satisfaction to our sense of justice and equity. It is a halting kind of justice which calls to the bar only the criminals of the beaten side and spares those in the victorious camp; and this is a disquieting fact. Undoubtedly it would be far better, as soon as possible, to entrust this vindicative function to a court instituted by the United Nations Organization.

Meanwhile, however regrettable be the defects of the existing structure, they do not invalidate the sentences passed upon the defendants really convicted of crimes. These persons have no ground to protest against the sentences which they have justly received simply because other guilty men have escaped the verdict. Further, it is clear that the first trials of major war criminals have dissipated many fears which were entertained about the strict impartiality of the Nuremberg Tribunal, owing to the full publicity given to the conduct of the trials, the ample facilities granted to the defence and the dignified bearing of the court.

(g) Another cause of anxiety, which is not unreasonable, relates to the use which an unjust victor could make of this precedent of vindicative justice against his beaten enemy. It is feared that the arm which has now been forged may be turned against those whose rights it is intended to defend.

Certainly, there is no human institution which cannot be abused, and the administration of justice is no exception. But nobody uses this argument to demand the suppression of all judicial institutions on the ground that unworthy judges are to be found. Besides, in the course of hostilities, a just belligerent does not always resist the temptation to have recourse to measures repugnant to morality and the laws of war. Fear of the just sanctions to which he renders himself liable will have a wholesale effect in persuading him to keep within the strict limits of morality and law.

(h) The adage *nulla poena sine lege* (no penalty should be imposed without a law providing for it) has been used as the basis of an argument to contest the right of an international tribunal to punish acts which had not, up to that time, been made subject to penalties by any positive law.

The saying thus invoked was meant to safeguard persons brought before a court from the arbitrary decision of a tyrannical authority; it has not the unqualified meaning which is often given it. It is not positive law which gives to an act which it prohibits its criminal character; it is the inherent malice of the act itself, and it is this that calls for punishment. The majority of war crimes amenable to international repression are, however, almost always contrary to the established law of the territories in which they have been perpetrated, the law which already exists to protect persons against unjust violence.

There are other criminal acts which infringe international laws and conventions relating to war, ratified by universal custom or by the formal consent of States. Aggressive war undertaken as an instrument of national policy was explicitly outlawed by the Briand-Kellogg Pact of August 27, 1928, ratified by some sixty States, which constituted the vast majority of the civilized world.

"Crimes against humanity" so violently outrage the consciences of all right-minded people and so evidently call for the sanctions of punitive justice that there is no need of any particular law to make them penal offences.

184. Of the four conditions the just victor can impose upon his vanquished enemy, *restitution,* which restores his impugned or violated right, is obviously the most important; it was the essential and immediate reason for undertaking the war. The fourth—*security*—has both for himself and for the collectivity of States, an importance equal to the first; war is made in order to obtain a lasting peace. *Reparations* and *sanctions* are not so much ends of war as means of reinforcing peace, and the victor must consider them primarily under that aspect when he makes up his list of demands.

185. There are two ways open to the just victor in providing for his security; he may either morally disarm the enemy and gain his esteem by the Christian moderation and meekness of the terms imposed, or make him physically incapable of renewing the struggle (by limitation of armaments, territorial annexations).

The first method is certainly more in conformity with the law of charity and must be preferred to the other when it is likely to result in a sincere and full reconciliation. It would be wrong to underestimate its efficacy, and history flatly contradicts on this point the opinion of prejudiced sceptics. But both parties are needed for reconciliation; the generous offer of the victor must be met by the open and sincere acceptance of the vanquished enemy. If the latter refuses to make this gesture or if his previous conduct leads one to doubt his promises, the victor has only one way left to provide for his security: namely, disarmament or territorial annexations.

186. In itself, there is nothing wrong in disarmament imposed on an unjust aggressor, as long as it does not leave the vanquished enemy defenceless against the eventual attack of a third power. But unless there is a general and simultaneous reduction of armaments, how can one prevent the State on whom this obligation is imposed from considering itself, rightly or wrongly, as being subject to some exterior menace and unjustly deprived of any means to counter it? On the other hand, the control implied by this sanction will either be illusory and useless, or inquisitorial to the point of being odious. It therefore seems that this measure is hardly likely to promote the re-establishment of peace and security.

187. All moralists have recognized the lawfulness of annexation which takes place on the grounds of reparations, sanctions or security. For if the victim of an unjust aggression is allowed to indemnify himself with the goods of the enemy, to punish the unjust aggressor and to prevent effectively the renewal of such attacks, there is no reason why the territory of the enemy should alone always escape the effects of such a right.

At the present day, however, annexation is less easily accepted as a legitimate condition of peace, and this attitude is supported by an argument which is not without weight. In former times, annexation involved far less disadvantages for the transferred populations than it does today. The very strong particularism of their local life lessened their consciousness of a true national unity, if it did not sometimes entirely obliterate it; the wide political decentralization then prevalent allowed them to change allegiance without losing their autonomy, and they accepted their fate quite readily. But in our modern unified and strongly centralized States, the loss of a province is a very painful amputation, and the conquered populations are very unwilling to submit to a transfer of sovereignty which is equivalent to complete denationalization. This inevitably creates Irredentisms, which in turn become sources of irreconcilable antagonisms and hardly serve the cause of peace, for which the war was made. Nowadays annexation can be only an extreme solution, except in very rare cases which concern provinces formerly belonging to the victor and which had been taken from him in previous disputes.

188. Such are the "aims of war" which the just belligerent may lawfully assign to his enterprise. It remains to be seen whether he may continue war until he gains a decisive victory which enables him to impose them upon his adversary, or whether he is bound to accept the pacific gestures of the enemy sooner.

The unjust aggressor who sees his chances of success diminishing will first of all try to make the best possible use of the advantages he may have gained at the beginning of the campaign. He will therefore begin by showing peaceful intentions and will even suggest the opening of negotiations, which the material advantages he still holds will allow him to exploit for his own ends. These first overtures cannot in themselves oblige a State which has a just cause for war to open negotiations with the enemy without delay. The latter must first of all give unmistakable proofs of the sincerity of his intentions. The just belligerent can quite rightly demand the restitution by the enemy of those advantages he wrongfully detains, and which can never form the subject of diplomatic negotiations.

189. Friendly mediators, who do not wish to judge the merits of the conflict, but are anxious to put an end to excessive bloodshed, often recommend a "blank peace" which will simply re-establish the *status quo ante bellum.* This proposal may be interpreted in two ways. If the just belligerent is asked to give up all his demands, including the restoration of his injured or violated rights, he is in no way obliged to accept it; if the "blank peace" implies merely the renunciation of reparations, sanctions or guarantees, justice, which demands that he should not require useless sacrifices from his own subjects, and charity, which he owes even to his enemies, may impose upon the just belligerent the duty of accepting it as a conciliatory form of settlement.

190. (a) Lastly, when the enemy offers to give complete satisfaction, the victor has no longer the right to continue the struggle. He can, however, make the suspension of hostilities conditional to the signature of an armistice which will render the enemy incapable of renewing the fight.

(b) An unjust aggressor, when he has lost the war, is inclined to urge that the treaty of peace imposed upon him is not valid, and to think that he is not bound by a *dictat*, the terms of which he has not been allowed to discuss. This is not a good argument. As long as the just belligerent keeps to his purpose of restoring the lawful order which has been unjustly disturbed, he is under no obligation to discuss this task with the enemy whom he has reduced to impotence. At the most, he is well-advised to hear and examine the objections which the defeated power considers that he must put forward to the terms imposed upon him.

It is a different matter when the just belligerent, who has failed to overcome the opposition of his enemy, resigns himself to conclude a peace of compromise with him. In that case the peace treaty is the outcome of negotiations in which the two parties take part on perfectly equal terms.

(c) As experience shows us, the treaties with which wars are concluded only too often contain within themselves the seeds of future conflicts, the vanquished nation denouncing the excessive burdens imposed upon it and the victor refusing to modify them in any way. It is well to take to heart the recommendations made by Pope Pius XII in his Christmas Message of 1939 in order to prevent such quarrels repeating themselves. He said:

"It is so difficult for human nature, if not practically impossible, to foresee everything and to be sure about every point at the moment when peace is being negotiated. It is very hard at that time to rid oneself completely of passion and bitterness. Therefore the establishment of juridical institutions, whose business it is to guarantee the loyal and faithful observance of conventions and, in case of recognized need, to revise and correct them, is of capital importance to ensure that a treaty is honourably accepted, and to avoid arbitrary and one-sided attempts to impair or interpret the conditions of the treaty itself."

(d) It may be objected that this measure proposed by the Holy Father, by opening the door to revision at a future date of the conditions of peace, gives a defeated nation the opportunity constantly to question the treaties which it has signed and thus seriously to compromise the stability of international relations. That is clearly not what Pope Pius XII recommends. The juridical institutions which he suggests are designed precisely "to guarantee the loyal and faithful observance of conventions"; revision must be undertaken only "in case of recognized need." It is an absolutely impartial body of arbitrators who would be called upon to give a decision when a demand for revision is put forward; if they considered that the demand was not well-founded, the party making the request would have the duty to accept this decision.

ii. *The Unjust Belligerent Is Victorious*

191. Victory does not confer any rights on the unjust belligerent; it is as iniquitous as all the acts of war which preceded it.

192. Nevertheless, when every reasonable hope of success has disappeared, justice may demand the just belligerent to spare his own subjects the prolongation of useless resistance and to accept the law of the victor, however heavy it may be.

In itself, the treaty imposed by an unjust belligerent is null and void; the force which has dictated it cannot create right. The vanquished belligerent is nevertheless obliged to accept it, not on account of the victor's right (since this right does not exist), but in the interests of his own subjects and of the international community which he must preserve from the horrors of another war.

It follows from the absolute nullity of the rights assumed by the unjust victor that the vanquished enemy may continue to hope for a legitimate revenge. He may also, when another conflict takes place (not provoked by him, but involving his enemy), put forward his claims and demand the restitution of those goods and territories of which he was unjustly despoiled.

VI. INTERVENTION AND NEUTRALITY

193. When a war breaks out between two States, the other powers, in the hypothesis of a still unorganized international society, have to choose between two courses: intervention and neutrality.

194. Intervention, as has already been said, is lawful only if it takes place on behalf of the belligerent who has a just cause for war.

It may sometimes become a strict obligation; it is an obligation of justice when a State has bound itself by treaty to assist another State unjustly attacked; it is an obligation of charity when exercised towards a State which is too weak to defend itself alone against unjust aggression and which can be helped without too much trouble.

Except in cases of contractual agreement, a State must first of all determine its attitude according to the true interests of the community under its care. This will often demand abstention from any kind of intervention.

195. Neutrality is the situation of a State which refuses to declare itself for either of the belligerents and forbids itself any interference in their quarrel.

It may be obligatory, either by virtue of a perpetual status (perpetual neutrality) or of a declaration made before the beginning of hostilities (occasional or voluntary neutrality).

Perpetual neutrality forbids any treaty of alliance and is as often as not imposed on a State for reasons of general interest; it admits of no exception.[25] The same cannot be said of occasional neutrality, for the latter cannot be allowed to prevail against an obligation of justice or of charity which would demand intervention in certain circumstances.

Neutrality is *conditional* when the State which proclaims it has taken care to lay down the terms on which it refrains from intervention.

It is *armed* when a State equips itself to defend its neutrality against any belligerent who might attempt to break it.

196. As long as a State refrains from taking part in the dispute, neither belligerent has the right to treat it as an enemy. Usually, neutrality is spontaneously declared at the beginning of hostilities. The parties at war are vitally interested in knowing from the very start what opposition they will have to reckon with. A belligerent has the right to ask very definite questions of a power which has not yet made known its intentions and whose eventual intervention it has reasons to fear, and to demand a declaration which does not leave room for ambiguous interpretation. A refusal to reply or an evasive answer would naturally lead to the suspicion of hostile ulterior motives, and authorizes the interpellator to take all means necessary for his defence.

197. Neutrality implies certain rights and duties which have taken a long time to define and codify. The task was not an easy one, for it meant the harmonizing of demands which are difficult to reconcile—those of neutrals who wish to keep their liberty of action in the face of a conflict which does not concern them, and those of belligerents

[25] In point of fact, Switzerland is the only State whose permanent neutrality is established by modern international law. The unique function exercised by the Swiss in regard to the Red Cross is made possible by that fact.

who will not allow this liberty to interfere unduly with their strategic activity or to become a source of advantage to the enemy.

The rights and duties of neutrals were made the subject of two conventions at the second Hague Conference (1907), the first concerning war on land and the second, naval war.

198. The duties imposed by neutrality are twofold; first of all, refusal to partake either directly or indirectly in the hostilities; secondly, to show absolute impartiality towards the belligerents. The neutral State cannot therefore place its territory at the disposal of the belligerents, or supply them with troops, arms, munitions, and the like. On the other hand, it must give equal treatment to the two parties at war in all the measures the dispute obliges it to take.

Nevertheless, these rules bind only the neutral States themselves; their subjects are still free to enlist—at their own risk—in the belligerent armies, to furnish them with supplies and so forth. It goes without saying that in conscience they can support only the adversary who has a just cause for war.

The neutral State may limit the exercise of this right and even forbid it absolutely. But if it takes this step, it must treat both belligerents equally.

This impartiality must be understood in a purely passive sense; the neutral State cannot do anything to favour one of the belligerents at the expense of the other. It is not active in this sense, that the neutral State is not bound to take any measures to ensure that the trade and help of its subjects are equally helpful to both States at war.

The neutral State is responsible for acts contrary to neutrality which it performs or allows to be performed on its territory and which it could have prevented, and is bound to make good the damage which its fault or negligence causes to the injured belligerent. If these infringements of neutrality are of a definitely hostile nature, they may even become a legitimate *casus belli.*

199. Within the limits of these obligations, the neutral State has a right to the inviolability of its territory, the respect of its independence, and the free exercise of international commerce. As regards the latter, however, the liberty demanded must be harmonized with that claimed by the belligerents for the effective conducting of war. Positive international law has tried to conciliate, especially as regards naval war, the legitimate demands of both parties (Second Hague Conference, 1907: *XIth Convention Relative to the Creation of an International Prize Court*).

   200. (a) As regards the immunity of neutral territory, history has witnessed a remarkable evolution of doctrine in the course of centuries.

Following St. Augustine, moralists have long held that "harmless transit through a territory must be allowed in view of the very equitable right of human society." *Transitus innocuus,* or harmless transit, is therefore an indubitable right which can be claimed by all members of the community of nations, as long as they pursue honest ends. A just belligerent is therefore justified in claiming it from a third power not concerned in the dispute. If the latter rejected his demand, it would be unjustly impeding the defensive action of the just belligerent, who would thereupon have the right of making his way through by force of arms.

From the point of view of the just belligerent, this interpretation is perfectly coherent and correct; but looked at from that of the third power in question, it gives rise to serious objections in practice. A State will often find it very difficult to decide whether the belligerent who asks for passage has a just cause for war. When it is doubtful, must he transform his territory into lists where the adversaries may settle their quarrel at their convenience? The whole doctrine of *transitus innocuus* is based on an unproved assumption. Were the theorists who propounded it ignorant of the fact that no country allowed peaceful passage to the rowdy and disorderly soldiery of the mercenary armies? On the other hand, the acceptance of the demand of one of the parties inevitably meant the risk of reprisals on the part of the other, who would use this permission to justify his own crossing of the frontiers of the over-hospitable State.

In order to harmonize more equitably the right of the just belligerent and the legitimate interests of neutrals, the severity of the doctrine of *transitus innocuus* has gradually been mitigated by opportune restrictions. But since the eighteenth century an entirely different idea has arisen among the lay theorists of the law of nations. They no longer consider war as a defensive action in the service of right; it is merely a trial of strength which, by mutual agreement, is to settle the dispute between the two adversaries. In this theory there is no longer any place for the doctrine of *transitus innocuus,* which is entirely based on the exclusive right of the just belligerent.

Thus has been constituted the modern theory of neutrality, of which the absolute immunity of neutral territory is but the necessary corollary.

(b) The absolute immunity of the neutral State's territory is the necessary corollary of the modern notion of neutrality. Consequently, the neutral State has the right to refuse permission, even to the forces of a just belligerent, to cross its territory. Even so, while neutrality can be morally justified on practical grounds arising from the unorganized condition of the international community, it has no place in a properly organized society of nations, which condemns unjust war as a crime against humanity and mobilizes the repressive action of all the other members of the society against a guilty belligerent. In these conditions, apart from the rare case of permanent neutrality formally accorded by the society itself to certain States, there is no territory for which such immunity can be claimed. The Charter of 1945, following the Covenant of the League of Nations, is perfectly logical in making it the duty of all members of the United Nations, when collective action is required, "to lend one another mutual assistance and the facilities necessary to maintain peace and international security, including the right of passage" (Art. 43, I).

(c) In recent times certain States have chosen an intermediate position between strict neutrality and open intervention. It is described as "non-belligerency" and it allows for a certain amount of assistance to one of the parties to the conflict. Other governments, yielding to the pressure of one of the belligerents, consent to grant facilities on their territory for the transport of his troops, munitions and supplies. They are within their right in so doing; but they act at their own risk and peril, for the other belligerent is entitled to resort to reprisals and counter-pressure in regard to them.

∗5∗

INTERNATIONAL SOCIETY ORGANIZED IN ACCORDANCE WITH NATURAL LAW AND THE CHRISTIAN ORDER

★★

I. INTRODUCTION

201. As has been shown above, there are two sorts of natural institutions. The first corresponds to an absolute and immediate need of human nature; the second is called for only when certain clearly defined conditions exist. The society of the family comes under the first head; under the second come the political society of the State and international society, for these become necessary only in given conditions arising from the density of population and the interdependence of societies.

The constitution of political societies or States has long become a reality in almost every part of the world. States have taken longer to realize how close is their solidarity and how necessary it is to give a lasting and definite status to the association which in fact exists between them.

202. After many unsuccessful attempts, the twentieth century has witnessed their endeavours to give a positive form to the natural society of States, finding expression in the Covenant of the League of Nations (1919) and the Charter of the United Nations (1945). For the conven-

163

ience of the reader, the latter document, to which the great majority of States have subscribed, is reproduced in Appendix II.

203. It is not for the science of ethics to define the precise form which the positive society of nations ought to take. Different opinions may quite legitimately be held about the method and the steps by which the desired end may be most effectively pursued at different stages in the historical evolution of mankind. However, it is possible and indeed necessary to establish the principles in accordance with which the value of an international institution can be judged and its improvement promoted.

II. INTERNATIONAL AUTHORITY AND ITS ORGANS

204. It has been shown above in Articles 13–28 that the natural society of nations, with the rights and duties which it involves, is an undoubted reality; the question is how to give it a positive juridical constitution.

In the present state of the world, it is only sovereign independent nations which are considered to be the formative elements of international society. That being so, there is no other way of giving this society a definite legal form than by freely accepted conventions and treaties.

205. But it must not be supposed that the assent of the nations is a prior requisite of the existence of this society; all that it can do is to furnish the society with the juridical equipment which it requires. The international society is not the product of the wills of men; it is an institution which corresponds to the imperative demands of human nature itself. Hence, since it has been created to promote the common good of the whole, it is necessarily preeminent over the States members who have agreed to give it practical form.

206. It is this pre-eminence which gives the interna-

tional society indisputable authority over the associated States. In order that this authority may be effectively exercised, it is necessary to designate persons to wield it. Only then is the positive society of States definitely constituted: for it is authority which gives any society its form.

207. All authority comes from God; but, apart from the society of the family, the Creator has left men free to choose the person or persons who are to exercise authority, and to determine the extent and the term of their mandate. Within the limits thus defined, persons invested with authority have the right to command, while the members of the society have the duty to obey.

208. The normal evolution of all political society naturally ends in a division of supreme authority between three powers—legislative, executive and judicial.

209. At the start, however, the authority resides wholly in the assembly or conference of representatives of the different governments concerned, who are presumed to exercise legitimate authority in their respective spheres.

Such is the conception of the Assembly of the former League of Nations and that of the present United Nations. This purely diplomatic gathering could, however, progressively transform itself into a real legislative assembly [1] empowered to deal, not with matters coming within the exclusive competence of each State, but with all questions of common interest, such as the maintenance of international order, economic co-operation for the common good,

---

[1] The international institution has not yet reached that stage of evolution. The General Assembly of the United Nations, like the Assembly of the old League, has power only to *recommend* to the members this or that action which it judges to be expedient, to adopt resolutions *ad referendum* or to draft conventions which the members remain free to ratify or not to ratify. The same is true of the commissions or specialized agencies responsible to the Assembly or associated with its work (see Articles 10 to 17 of the Charter).

the progress of social justice or the development of international exchanges and means of communication.

210. It is, further, a logical requirement of the effective working of the international society that it should have a smaller, less cumbersome, executive organ, whose members, within the limits of the mandate conferred upon them, have the power to *decide*, act and give orders in the name of the society as a whole. The principal purpose of the powers vested in this executive authority is to see to it that justice reigns—that is, to ensure by means of remonstrance, economic pressure or military constraint that the obligations assumed by the members of the society are respected, and that the decisions of the international judicial authority are obeyed. It should be empowered to prevent any aggression, either by a State outside the international society or by one or more of its member States.[2]

211. To that end the executive organ or council of the society, like any government within its own sphere, must have at its immediate disposal adequate police forces and must have authority, in case of necessity, to require member States to support its military action.[3] It is also highly desirable that it should be entrusted with the

[2] In this respect the United Nations Charter goes further than the Covenant of the League of Nations, in theory at least; for it gives the Security Council more extensive powers than were conferred upon the Council of the League (see Articles 24–26 and 39–51 of the Charter).

[3] Articles 43 and 45 of the Charter recognize these requirements. In fact, no result has been achieved by the General Staffs' Committee, and no agreement has been concluded between the Security Council and the various members concerning the military contingents which they will hold at the Council's disposal. (The precedent, however, of the military action undertaken by the Security Council in 1950 against aggression in Korea—made possible by the temporary absence of the Soviet delegate—and of the active co-operation of a number of members in this action, is of great historical importance in the evolution of the positive society of nations.)

direct control, if not with the actual ownership, of every institution concerned with the production of atomic energy.

212. The best way to harmonize the action of the Assembly, as the legislative organ, and that of the Council, as the executive, would be to entrust the former with the choice of those who are to be members of the latter. That choice should fall upon eminent personalities, of recognized integrity and competence, capable of devoting themselves with absolute loyalty to the interests of the international community.[4] As long as the members of this executive organ are no more than representatives of their governments, answerable to the national authorities who have appointed them, they will always be unable to exercise effectively the supreme power with which they have been invested; their agreement will be precarious, their hold upon the consciences of men uncertain. This state of affairs may be justified as a necessary expedient at the beginning of the endeavour to organize a world now imbued with an exaggerated notion of national sovereignty; it is indefensible on ideal and logical grounds.

213. In the same way, the fact that certain powers were accorded permanent seats on the Council can be justified as a provisional measure, on the ground that power must be in proportion to responsibilities. But it is quite incompatible with the ideal conception of international authority, that each of the great powers should have the right to veto every decision of the Council concerning the maintenance of peace, the admission of new members and amendments to the Charter of the society. The equality

[4] This principle has been followed in the election of the members of the International Court of Justice; but it was not adopted when the constitution of the Security Council was framed.

of all the members is an essential requirement of the reign of justice within that society.[5]

214. A real international society must necessarily have an independent judicial authority, whose duty it is to apply international law and to interpret treaties, in conformity with the general principles of natural law and equity. Further, since national sovereignty can never be absolute and the welfare of individual men and women constitutes the ultimate end both of the States themselves and of the community of States, the competence of the international society, and in particular of its Court of Justice ought to extend to the protection of the essential rights of man, which rights should themselves be guaranteed by international conventions.[6] Recourse to the jurisdiction of this supreme Court and acceptance of its verdicts ought to be obligatory and not merely optional. Enforcement measures would lawfully be put into action by the executive authority of the society against any State refusing to comply with its verdicts.[7]

[5] It is the granting of a right of veto to each of the great powers which has condemned the Security Council of the United Nations to sterility (except in the one case when, the Soviet delegate being absent, it was able to organize armed opposition to aggression in Korea).

[6] See the Universal Declaration of Human Rights adopted by the General Assembly of the United Nations in December, 1948, which, it is intended, will be followed by a binding covenant or international convention on the same subject. As an example of Catholic requirements in this regard, the Declaration of Rights submitted to the United Nations by the National Catholic Welfare Council on February 2, 1947 is reproduced in Appendix III.

[7] The Statute of the International Court of Justice empowers the judges to apply, in addition to existing treaties, "the general principles of law recognized by civilized nations," but it gives no definition of them. Only States can be parties to cases coming before the Court; and the Court can give an advisory opinion at the request of a member or of an organ of the United Nations. Acceptance of the Court's jurisdiction is optional.

III. The Problem of Universality

215. Because all the elements which make up the great family of mankind form a real natural society, all the States, into which that family is divided, are under an obligation to join the positive international society as members, as soon as it is possible to organize it. This universal character of the society is the ideal from the standpoint both of right reason and of the Christian tradition; but it does not follow that it can be immediately realized. There is an even more vital condition of the extent and efficacity of the positive society of States; and that is that all the affiliated governments must acknowledge those essential obligations of the moral law which are the foundation of all well-ordered social life.

216. Indeed, unless the essential *principle of sociability* be admitted, a government's acceptance of the obligations resulting from its membership will be no more than empty words and will always lack sincerity; its presence within the society will always tend to destroy its unity.

This principle of sociability involves two fundamental propositions. The first is that each State is only a part of a larger whole and that, in consequence, the common good of the whole must prevail over the interests of the parts. The second is that relations between the different States and between each of them and the international community must be strictly governed by the moral law, which demands above all things good faith and loyalty to the pledged word: *Pacta sunt servanda*—Promises must be kept.

217. Only too often nations and governments have disregarded the necessary primacy of the common good and

have insolently violated the most imperative requirements of the moral law. For all that, all the efforts which have been made throughout the course of history to organize international life and to keep the peace, up to and including the formation of the League of Nations and the United Nations, have always been inspired by a deep conviction of the solidarity of the nations; and that fact itself derives from the memory of the original unity of Christendom.

The progressive secularization of diplomacy has certainly gone very far to sap the moral foundations upon which all international collaboration is built. But it has not quite succeeded in destroying these foundations; for they are grounded in the natural reason and conscience of mankind, which it is and has always been the function of Christianity to elucidate and to defend.

218. It follows that in countries where the citizens enjoy enough liberty to discuss these matters, to express their views and to know about what is happening outside their own frontiers, public opinion can, to some extent, influence the government, urge it to bring its policy into line with what reason and conscience naturally demand, and prevent it from following a policy of immoral aggrandizement. That is one of the principal merits of democracy, rightly understood.

219. Very different is the condition of the totalitarian State. There, power is in the arbitrary hands of one party, which stifles or completely suppresses liberty of opinion, prevents citizens from having any free intercourse with peoples of other countries, and mobilizes the entire resources of the nation, both spiritual and material, to serve ends which are absolutely incompatible with the postulates of the natural solidarity of States—namely, the extension of its own power in the name of the supposed

rights of race, nationality or class. Any government which is based upon so frankly immoral and antisocial a principle and which is without the control of a free public opinion, has no place in the organized international society. If it be admitted to a part in the society's life, it will never cease to be an element of weakness and confusion. To give such a government a privileged position in the community of nations and to allow it, by the use of the veto, to block any collective action of the society, is to condemn the latter to incurable paralysis.

220. Thus, neither reason nor practical experience allows us to envisage the possibility of making the society of nations, at the start, absolutely universal. The wider the area which is under the rule of international law, the more securely can order and peace be maintained in the world. But as long as powerful antisocial forces are at their baneful work, the surest way to prevent aggression and war is to establish a system of effective solidarity among the greatest possible number of States who *do* respect the essential obligations of international society. This solidarity, finding expression in a partial society of States, does not mean that the natural and Christian ideal of universality has been thrown overboard; on the contrary, every effort must be made to achieve it as soon as possible. This close union by no means implies an offensive against any government whose principles render it unfit for international collaboration; for war will always remain the last and least desirable means of fighting ideas. Nor need it prevent economic and social relations with such a State and its subjects. The sole purpose of the allied States should be to refuse anything which might compromise the essential principles on which international co-operation is founded and, should the need arise, to de-

fend in common the fundamental rights of men and nations.

221. Realizing the inevitable defects of international society, resulting from the imperfections of our sadly divided world, all men of good will—and, most of all, Christian people—ought to adopt a constructive attitude. They should seize every opportunity to stand up for the right principles of international life and to combat erroneous notions opposed to them. Insofar as they are able, they should give their effective support to the activities of the international society, whose divers organs and technical commissions offer a wide field for their good will—the defence of essential human rights, the more sensible organization of the production and distribution of goods, financial reconstruction, the development of international co-operation on a continental and international scale, the improvement of conditions of labour, the prevention of disease, and relief work of all kinds.

222. Within the national life, all good citizens ought to support their rulers' endeavours to make continual improvement in the existing international organization; or, should that organization prove to be unequal to its task, to work out a plan for one which would be more in conformity with natural law and the Christian tradition.

IV. The Church and the International Society

223. It is a matter of particular interest to Catholics to determine what relationship could exist between the international society, were it organized in accordance with the principles which we have established above, and the Holy See. Even if all the world consisted of Christian nations, it would cause an unfortunate confusion between the spiritual and temporal powers if the papacy were

assigned a place in the councils of the international society. As Vicar of the Prince of Peace, it is the duty of the Sovereign Pontiff, whenever the changing circumstances of human life require it, to proclaim the true requirements of natural justice and Christian charity and to warn the nations against ideas and theories which are destructive of the moral order. As the Father of all Christians, his position and influence as a peacemaker would be seriously compromised if, through his representatives, he became involved in the political, economic and technical debates which must necessarily occupy the attention of the organs of the international society.

224. Apart from the beneficent influence of his spiritual magisterium, there are, however, three ways in which cooperation between the head of the Church on earth and the international society might be effected.

> 1. The Holy Father, as an independent moral authority, might place his good offices at the disposal of the international society, for the peaceful settlement of a dispute whenever the contending parties asked for his mediation or arbitration and agreed to accept his recommendations or his arbitral award. The history of the whole Christian era abounds in cases of papal intervention to preserve or restore peace.

> 2. Without prejudice to the legitimate independence both of the Church and of the international authority within their respective spheres, diplomatic relations could be established between them, so that the two powers might be kept mutually informed about their respective proposals and intentions in matters of common concern.

3. Finally, the Holy Father's co-operation could always be sought and given, within his means, in all humanitarian activities undertaken by the society of nations to relieve distress and to cope with great calamities.

·6·

INTERNATIONAL MORALITY AND THE
INDIVIDUAL CONSCIENCE

★★★

I. INTRODUCTION

225. Upon rulers, first and foremost, falls the responsibility of seeing to it that all the activities of the society which they are appointed to govern are in conformity with the precepts of international morality. But it is nonetheless necessary that the subjects should observe the same law of social justice and charity by assisting the rulers in their efforts and obeying their commands.

Since the national will, with which all governments, even the most despotic, have to reckon nowadays, is formed by the union of the individual wills of all the citizens, it is most important that each one should fully understand his international responsibilities. According to whether it is more or less enlightened, public opinion will be able to confine public authority within just limits, or will lead it, often against its will, to transgress the rules of international law.

This Code of international ethics would therefore be incomplete if, after enumerating the duties of rulers, it made no mention of the obligations of their subjects.

226. When faced with the problems of international life, the Christian must determine his judgements, his

acts, and his whole attitude according to the precepts of justice and charity, which are the essential basis of all well-ordered human relationships.

He will succeed only if he can achieve a true conciliation of two apparently contradictory tendencies: nationalism and internationalism; in other words, if he can hold the balance between what the undeniable unity of the human race demands of him and the regard which he ought to have for those most varied forms which that same humanity assumes in concrete reality.

227. The great principle of order which governs both national and international life is that the common good must always take precedence over the particular good. It is this same rule which makes it possible to reconcile fairly the requirements of nationalism and of internationalism, however difficult to adjust they may seem at first sight.

Nationalism and internationalism are terms which can be interpreted in very different ways and it is important to define clearly what one means by them.[1]

II. NATIONALISM

228. In one sense of the word, nationalism is closely connected with patriotism, without, however, having exactly the same meaning. Patriotism is a moral virtue which leads us to love our country, and to render all the duties prescribed by filial piety towards all those who have some claim to be responsible for our existence. The first thing which patriotism leads us to venerate is our ancestral land (*terra patria, vaderland, vaterland, country*), which we love, not for its own sake (we love our

---

[1] "It is evident that the parts are ordained to the perfection of the whole; the whole, indeed, does not exist for the parts; it is the parts which are made for the whole" (Saint Thomas: *Contra Gentiles,* III, Ch. CXII, 5).

country, whether it is great or small, rich or poor, according as nature has made it), but because it is the cradle of our race, because it gave us birth, because it is the home in which we share the thoughts and feelings of men of the same blood and culture.

Nationalism is concerned primarily with this community of race and blood (*nasci*: to be born); it is not necessarily confined to the territories of the State; for Irredentist nations, it exists beyond the frontiers. It is even found in nations which have no fatherland, such as the nomadic peoples and the Jews.

Even when it most closely resembles patriotism, nationalism may still be distinguished from it by its more vigilant concern to strengthen the bonds which exist between people of the same nation and to proclaim the undeniable priority of the common good over the interests of classes or parties. For it is when internal dissensions threaten to divide the social body and imperil its very existence that patriotism changes into nationalism and endeavours to rally all good citizens around a programme of unity and concord.

229. In countries where several nationalities are to be found, nationalism sometimes opposes itself to patriotism; national minorities wish to detach themselves from the common fatherland, and claim the right to dispose freely of their new autonomy. We have seen elsewhere the moral judgement to be passed on these separatist tendencies (see Art. 15).

230. Nationalism and patriotism do not confine their activity to the internal life of the country; both have an external aspect which brings them into contact, and often into conflict, with similar passions which hold sway over neighbouring nations.

Since it is the duty of the State to ensure the prosperity

of its subjects, patriotism claims that it has the right to fulfil this task with full independence and to take a large share in the advantages offered by international life. Nationalism adds the duty of maintaining, developing and spreading those traits and characteristics which belong to the temperament and specific genius of the nation.

231. In itself this double preoccupation is perfectly legitimate. Since nature has entrusted this mission to the State, the latter has undoubtedly the right to seek its accomplishment with full independence and responsibility within the wider framework of international society.

On the other hand, it is a fact, willed by the Author of nature Himself, that humanity, in itself a unity, should be diversified in individuals and societies according to heredity, natural and social surroundings, education and customs. The traits and characteristics which constitute a nationality are therefore natural values which each national group has the right to maintain, enrich and defend against any attempt at assimilation or absorption.

232. Though nationalism is a good and sound thing in itself, it becomes a lawless and baneful passion when national culture, which is truly valuable and important, is made an absolute value.

Exaggerated nationalism does not hesitate to sacrifice the cultural values of other nations to this relative value which it has arbitrarily made absolute; it will even claim to subordinate to itself the transcendental and universal notions of right, morality, truth and religion.

233. When nationalism has reached this pitch, it can no longer be reconciled with the precepts of right and Christian ethics.

III. INTERNATIONALISM

234. Internationalism, when kept within just limits, is an effective antidote to excessive nationalism. But here

again we must avoid exaggeration. Internationalism may also have a good and a bad meaning.

235. The fervent support given by Socialists and Communists to internationalism has greatly helped to discredit both the term and the reality in Catholic circles and not altogether without reason, since internationalism thus patronized implies the suppression of frontiers, the abolition of nationalities, making the world a vast battleground in which a merciless class war will replace national antagonisms. This idea has been a useful instrument of Marxist propaganda, but it is utterly chimerical, since it ignores the natural law of differentiation which will ever continue to endow each nation with special characteristics.

236. There is another internationalism which we would rather call—if usage allowed—*universalism*, so as to emphasize the sense in which it complements the particularism of nations.

This type of internationalism does not disdain the very diverse cultural values which distinguish the various national groups and form their heritage. It respects them fully, for it knows their worth. But it goes beyond these contingent aspects of human life to discover and retain as a higher reality that identity of nature which makes all human beings to be members of one family, and all nations the constituent parts of a much vaster, supranational, universal society.

Since they are equally based on the demands of human nature, particular societies and universal society, far from being mutually exclusive, have a need of one another for their mutual completion. The national societies must find their place in international society, without being absorbed by it. They remain responsible for the common good of their subjects, but must subordinate this special good to the universal good, which is the specific end of international society.

IV. A Just Synthesis

237. From the ethical point of view, there is no absolute opposition between national duty and international duty. A Christian must and can fulfil both, following the example of the Church, whose wonderful catholicity includes the salvation of individuals, the prosperity of nations and the good of humanity in its universal solicitude.

Man must not separate in his affections the particular society into which he was born and the human family to which he belongs by nature. The love he bears his country will be one of preference, not an exclusive passion, since that country could not prosper apart from, or in conflict with, the higher good of universal society. Devoted attachment to his country should make him desire its sincere collaboration in the task of achieving this higher good, and the subordination of its own particular ends to this good, for their better safeguard.

Thus will the Christian conscience harmonize in a perfect synthesis the equally well-founded demands of nationalism and internationalism, of national particularism and human universalism.

V. Education of Public Opinion

238. It is not enough to win the support of a cultured minority for the principles of international morality. For at a time of crisis, when national passions are inflamed, there is only too much danger that its voice will be lost in the uproar. It is the masses of the people who must be converted to a healthier understanding of the requirements of international life. This demands a powerful edu-

cational effort, for which certain groups of citizens have a special responsibility.

239. Teachers have a very important task to fulfil in this respect. It is certainly their duty to foster in their pupils those ideals and virtues which will make them good and loyal citizens; but they are also bound to teach them the duties resulting from international solidarity. To this effect they will endeavour to inculcate a knowledge and appreciation of the qualities of other nations; they will stress the close interdependence of peoples; they will especially point out the benefits of concord and peace. As objective and impartial interpreters of historical events, they will avoid anything which is likely to foster false prejudices, keep up enmities, or enkindle hatred.

240. The school can only begin this work of education; it must be unremittingly pursued by those who have undertaken the very responsible task of enlightening and guiding public opinion. In this regard the press is a powerful method of propaganda, which should not be allowed to support indiscriminately every kind of national cause.

Christian publicists, realizing the greatness and the nobility of their profession, ought to make it their duty to treat with absolute objectivity the great controversies which divide nations, eschewing all unjustifiable accusations and all injurious expressions which might embitter the quarrel, and taking care themselves both to understand and to explain to their readers the point of view of the other side.[2]

---

[2] Pope Pius XII has vigorously condemned the excesses into which too many publicists are betrayed by a passionate nationalism and has shown Catholic writers where their true duty lies. "At the present time there is in progress, in certain countries, an unbridled propaganda, which does not hesitate to make flagrant perversions of the truth in order, day by day and almost hour by hour, to show the opposing

241. Priests have a most special duty, as the messengers of the God of peace, to work without ceasing for the conversion of minds and hearts, so that the peace of Christ which we ardently desire, the "reign of peace, justice and love," [3] may at last prevail over the dissensions of the human race. This great and noble task was given them by Pope Benedict XV when he wrote to his brethren in the episcopate: "It is Our especial wish that you should exhort your priests, as the ministers of peace, to be assiduous in urging this love of one's neighbour and even of enemies which is the essence of the Christian life and, by being all things to all men and giving an example to others, wage war everywhere on enmity and hatred" (*Pacem Dei munus*).

242. The world cannot give humanity that peace which it so greatly desires: it is "the most beautiful gift of God" (*Ibid.*). Therefore, in answer to the call of Pope Pius XI, "all Christian peoples must pray fervently and unanimously to God, who holds in His hands the hearts of rulers, that He may inspire all with *thoughts of peace and not of affliction* [4] and, together with these thoughts, the firm purpose to put them into action and the strength to make them successful.

"Thus," adds Pius XI, "for the great consolation of all, shall we see the fulfilment of the prayer which the Church

nations to public opinion in a false and damaging light. Those who really desire the welfare of the people, those who want to help preserve from incalculable damage the spiritual and moral bases upon which the peoples may once more collaborate in the future—such men ought to consider it a sacred duty and a noble task *not* to allow the natural ideals of truthfulness, justice, good manners and co-operation for the common good, and especially the sublime and supernatural ideal of brotherly love brought into this world by Christ, to be lost in the thoughts and feelings of men" (Christmas Message, 1940).

[3] Preface of the Feast of Christ the King.

[4] Jerem. 29:11.

places on the lips of her ministers in the sacred liturgy: *'Grant, O Lord, we beseech Thee, that the course of the world may be peaceably ordered for us by Thy providence, and that Thy Church may rejoice in quiet devotion'* [5] (Letter *Quando nel principio*, to Cardinal Gasparri, June 24, 1923).

[5] Collect of the Fourth Sunday after Pentecost.

POPE PIUS XII AND
INTERNATIONAL MORALITY

****

On very many occasions during the Second World War His Holiness Pope Pius XII recalled and gave precision to the eternal principles of justice, charity and solidarity, upon which depend the peace and prosperity of the world. The various documents in which the Pope has expressed his thoughts on these subjects themselves furnish the elements of an imposing *Summa* of Christian international law. It would not have been difficult to reinforce almost all the articles of this Code with quotations from the wartime messages of the Pope. But we feel that the wealth of this clear and vigorous teaching would be diminished were it cut up and scattered all through this work of ours. We prefer to reproduce as a whole those passages in which His Holiness has himself condensed his doctrine with admirable conciseness. The reader will find in them a splendid synthesis of the principles formulated in this Code of international ethics.

I. Extracts From the Encyclical *Summi Pontificatus*
(October 20, 1939)

As nations become more civilized, they become more highly differentiated in their ways of living and of managing their affairs. That is no reason why they should renounce the unity of the human family. Rather, they should enrich that family by making their own contribution to its variety, according to their several endowments. They should exchange, mutually, the advantages they enjoy; and that is a thing which can be done satisfactorily only where a lively, burning charity unites us all in a common brotherhood, as sons of the same Father and men redeemed by the same divine Blood.

The Church of Jesus Christ is the repository of His wisdom; she is certainly too wise to discourage or belittle those peculiarities and differences which mark out one nation from another. It is quite legitimate for nations to treat those differences as a sacred inheritance and guard them at all costs. The Church aims at unity, a unity determined and kept alive by that supernatural love which should be actuating everybody; she does not aim at a uniformity which would be only external in its effects and would cramp the natural tendencies of the nations concerned. Every nation has its own genius, its own qualities, springing from the hidden roots of its being. The wise development, the encouragement within limits, of that genius and those qualities, does no harm; and if a nation cares to take precautions to lay down rules for that end, it has the Church's approval. She is mother enough to befriend such projects with her prayers, as long as all is done without prejudice to those duties which the common origin and the common destiny of the whole human race impose upon us.

State-Worship and International Confidence

This erroneous notion, Worshipful Brethren, which assigns unlimited powers to the State, is not only fatal to the internal life of a society and to its chances of healthy progress; it is equally disastrous to the relations of peoples with one another. It breaks the bonds which ought to unite commonwealths; it robs international law of all its vigour; it makes States almost incapable of living together on terms of peace and good will.

Mankind, by a divinely appointed law, is divided into a variety of classes; by the same law, it is divided into a variety of peoples and States. These do not depend on one another as far as the ordering of their internal affairs is concerned. But they are bound by mutual obligations in law and in moral right; they form a vast community of nations which is designed to promote the general good of the race. They are governed by special rules which preserve unity amongst them and advance, from day to day, their happiness.

It must be manifest to everybody that the claim of absolute, irresponsible powers for the governing body in the State is inimical to this ingrained law of our nature, and summarily rejects it. Such powers, it is equally plain, put all the bonds which unite one country with another at the mercy of a capricious despotism. They leave no room for honest agreement between men's minds and for the organization of mutual assistance. Nothing else is demanded, Worshipful Brethren, by any international understanding which is to be properly guaranteed and reasonably secure of permanence, nothing else is demanded by the need for fruitful alliances, than a due recognition of the basic principles of international law and a determination to abide by them. And these principles enjoin that each nation shall be allowed to keep its own liberties intact, shall have the right to its own life and economic development; further, they enjoin that any pact which has been solemnly ratified in accordance with the rights of nations shall persist, unimpaired and inviolable.

If nations are to live at peace together, if they are to be

bound by clearly defined obligations to one another, the first requisite is mutual confidence. There must be general persuasion that an oath given will be kept sacred by both parties, a general acceptance of the maxim that "wisdom is a better thing than weapons of war." [1] Moreover, all must be prepared to have their case looked into and discussed at leisure, instead of betaking themselves hurriedly to violence or threats as the solution of the difficulty—and this especially where delays, disputes, problems, changes of front have hindered the progress of negotiation, since such obstacles do not always arise from bad faith but are often due to changed circumstances or an unexpected clash of interests.

It is clear enough what is meant when the rights of nations are altogether excluded from the scope of the divine law, and made to depend on the caprice of individual rulers as their sole sanction. It means that those rights are being dethroned from all the estimation, from all the security which they enjoy, and are being left at the disposal of hasty minds, intent on public or private advantage, dominated by no other motive than to assert their own rights and reject those of others.

This reservation must always be made, that in the course of time new situations may arise which were not foreseen and perhaps could not be foreseen at the time when the pact was made. In that case, either the whole agreement or some part of it may have become, or may seem to have become, unjust to one of the contracting parties; or there may be undertakings which now would bear too hardly upon that party or be altogether impossible of fulfilment. In such a case, the obvious expedient is to take refuge as soon as possible in a full and frank discussion of the difficulty, so that the old pact can

[1] Eccles. 9:18.

be suitably altered or a new pact substituted for it. It is quite a different thing to regard all signed pacts as written in water, assuming to oneself the tacit right of breaking them at one's own discretion, whenever self-interest demands it, without consulting or without having any regard for the other contracting party. Such behaviour can only deprive nations of the spirit of confidence which ought to exist between them. It is utterly subversive of the natural order, and leaves nations and peoples severed from one another by deep rivers of distrust.

II. Extracts From the Christmas Message, 1939

i. *National Independence* [2]

A fundamental postulate of any just and honourable peace is an assurance for all nations great or small, powerful or weak, of their right to life and independence. The will of one nation to live must never mean the sentence of death passed upon another. When this equality of rights has been destroyed, attacked or threatened, order demands that reparation shall be made; and the measure and extent of that reparation is determined, not by the sword nor by the arbitrary decision of self-interest, but by the rules of justice and reciprocal equity.

ii. *Limitation of Armaments*

The order thus established, if it is to continue undisturbed and ensure true peace, requires that the nations be delivered from the slavery imposed upon them by the race for armaments, and from the danger that material force, instead of serving to protect the right, may become an overbearing and tyrannical master. Any peaceful settlement which fails to give fundamental importance to a

[2] The crossheads have been inserted.

mutually agreed, organic and progressive disarmament, spiritual as well as material, or which neglects to ensure the effective and loyal implementing of such an agreement, will sooner or later show itself to be lacking in coherence and vitality.

iii. *Juridical Revision of Treaties*

The maxims of human wisdom require that in any reorganization of international life all parties should learn a lesson from the failures and deficiencies of the past. Hence in creating or reconstructing international institutions which have so high a mission and such difficult and grave responsibilities, it is important to bear in mind the experience gained from the ineffectiveness or imperfections of previous institutions of the same kind. Human frailty renders it difficult, not to say impossible, to foresee every contingency and guard against every danger at the moment in which treaties are signed; passion and bitter feeling are likely to be still rife. Hence, in order that a peace may be honourably accepted and in order that arbitrary breaches and unilateral interpretations of treaties may be avoided, it is of the first importance to erect some juridical institution which shall guarantee the loyal and faithful fulfilment of the conditions agreed upon and which shall, in case of recognized need, revise and correct them.

iv. *Regard for Minorities*

If a better European settlement is to be reached, there is one point in particular which should receive special attention: it is the real needs and the just demands of nations and populations and of racial minorities. It may be that, in consequence of existing treaties incompatible with them, these demands are unable to establish a strictly legal right. Even so, they deserve to be examined in a friendly spirit with a view to meeting them by peaceful methods, and even, where it appears necessary, by means of an equitable and covenanted revision of the treaties themselves. If the balance between nations is thus adjusted and the foundation of mutual confidence is thus laid, many incentives to violent action will be removed.

v. *Supremacy of the Moral Law*

But even the best and most detailed regulations will be imperfect and foredoomed to failure unless the peoples and those who govern them submit willingly to the influence of that spirit which alone can give life, authority, and binding force to the dead letter of international agreements. They must develop that sense of deep and keen responsibility which measures and weighs human statutes according to the sacred and inviolable standards of the law of God. They must cultivate that hunger and thirst after justice which is proclaimed as a beatitude in the Sermon on the Mount and which supposes as its natural foundation the moral virtue of justice. They must be guided by that universal love which is the compendium and most general expression of the Christian ideal, and which therefore throws a bridge even towards those who have not the blessing of sharing the same Faith with us.

III. EXTRACTS FROM THE CHRISTMAS MESSAGE, 1940

Five Conditions of Peace

[The necessary premises for a new order of the world such as the Pope postulates are as follows:]

i. Victory over the hatred which divides the nations today, and the disappearance of systems and actions which breed this hatred. As a matter of fact, in some countries an unbridled propaganda is to be seen; it does not recoil from methodical distortion of the truth in order to show the enemy nations in a falsified and vilifying light. He, however, who really wants the good of the people and wants to contribute to the future co-operation of nations and to preserve this co-operation from incalculable damage, will consider it as his sacred duty to uphold the natural ideals of truth, justice and charity.

ii. Victory over distrust, which exerts a paralyzing pressure on international law and makes all honest understanding impossible. Therefore, return to the principle of mutual trust. Return to the loyalty for treaties without which the secure co-operation of nations and especially the living side by side of strong and weak nations are inconceivable. The foundation of justice is loyalty, reliability, and truth of the pledged word and of the understanding which has been reached.

iii. Victory over the dismal principle that utility is the foundation and aim of law and that might can create right. This principle is certain to upset all international relations and is inacceptable to all weaker nations. Therefore, return to honest, serious and moral international relations. This conception does not exclude the desire for the honourable improvement of conditions or the right to defend oneself if peaceful life has been attacked, or to repair the damage sustained thereby.

iv. Victory over those potential conflicts arising out of the disequilibrium of world economy. Therefore, a new economic order has to be gradually evolved which gives all nations the means to secure for their citizens an appropriate standard of life.

v. Victory over the kind of egoism which, relying on its own power, aims at impairing the honour and sovereignty of nations as well as the sound, just and ordered liberty of individuals. This egoism has to be replaced by a genuine Christian solidarity of a legal and economic character, and by a brotherly co-operation of the nations, the sovereignty of which has been duly secured.

IV. EXTRACTS FROM THE CHRISTMAS MESSAGE, 1941

i. *The Freedom, Integrity and Security of Other Nations* [3]

Within the framework of a new order based upon moral principles, there is no room for the violation of the freedom, integrity, and security of other nations, whatever be their territorial extent or their capacity for defence. If it is inevitable that the great States should, by reason of their greater resources and their power, lead the way in forming economic groups between themselves and the smaller and weaker nations, nevertheless what holds for all in the sphere of the common interest holds also for these smaller nations: that they possess an unquestionable right to have their political freedom respected—a right to the effectual safeguarding of that neutrality in conflicts between other States which belongs to them in virtue of the natural law and the law of nations, and a right to the protection of their economic development. Only in such circumstances can they adequately secure the material and spiritual well-being of their respective peoples.

ii. *The Observance of the Rights of Minorities*

Within the framework of a new order based upon moral principles, there is no room for the suppression, be it open or covert, of the cultural and linguistic traditions of national minorities, for the obstruction or restriction of their economic capacity, or for the limitation or destruction of their natural resources. The more conscientiously the competent authority of the State respects the rights of minorities, the more confidently and effectually will it be

[3] Crossheads have been inserted.

able to demand from their members the loyal discharge of those civic duties which they have in common with the other citizens.

iii. *Access to Raw Materials*

Within the framework of a new order based upon moral principles, there is no room for that narrow and calculating egoism which tends to monopolize economic sources and materials of common use, to the exclusion of nations less naturally favoured. In this connection, We are very greatly consoled to find that the necessity of a common sharing in the goods of the earth is affirmed even by those nations which, in the implementing of this principle, would belong to the category of givers and not of receivers. But equity requires that a solution of this question so decisive for world economy should be reached methodically, gradually, and with the necessary guarantees, due regard being paid to the lessons which past failures and omissions have to teach. A refusal to face this problem courageously in the future peace settlement would leave in international relations the deep and spreading root of bitter grievances and jealous animosities which would finally result in a renewal of the conflict. It is to be observed, however, that a satisfactory agreement on this point is closely connected with another cardinal requirement of the new order, of which We speak in the next paragraph.

iv. *The Limitation of Armaments*

Within the framework of a new order based upon moral principles, there is no room (when the most dangerous breeding-grounds of conflict have once been eliminated) for total warfare or for a reckless race for armaments. Not for the third time must the misfortune of a world war, with its economic and social havoc, its moral turmoil and aberrations, be allowed to afflict humanity. If the human race is to be preserved from the repetition of such a scourge, it will be necessary honestly and seriously to take steps for a gradual and adequate limitation of armaments. The disproportion between the excessive armament of powerful States and the inadequate armament of weak nations creates a threat to the peace and tranquillity of peoples, and points to the wisdom of reducing the manufacture and storing of offensive weapons to a limit of sufficiency and proportion.

Conformably to the measure in which such disarmament takes place, appropriate means, honourable to all parties and at the same time efficacious, should be taken to ensure for the axiom "Pacts must be observed" that vital moral function which belongs to it in juridical relations between States. In the past this axiom has been sorely imperilled and undeniably infringed, and has been confronted by an almost incurable distrust among peoples and their respective rulers. To bring about the rebirth of reciprocal confidence, institutions must be established which will command universal respect and will devote themselves to the noble task, both of guaranteeing the sincere implementing of treaties and also, where the principles of justice and equity require it, of bringing about opportune corrections and revisions of their conditions.

V. Extracts From the Christmas Message, 1942

i. *The Dignity and Rights of the Human Person* [4]

He who would have the star of peace to shine permanently over society must do all in his power to restore to the human person the dignity which God conferred upon

---

[4] Crossheads have been inserted.

him from the beginning. He must resist the excessive herding together of human beings, as though they were a soulless mass. He must set his face against their disintegration in economic, social, political, intellectual, and moral life; against their lack of solid principles and firm convictions; against their excessive reliance upon instinct and emotion, and against their fickleness of mood. He must favour, by all legitimate means and in every sphere of life, social forms which render possible and guarantee full personal responsibility in regard to things both temporal and spiritual.

He must foster the observance and practical implementing of the following fundamental rights of the person: the right to maintain and develop physical, intellectual, and moral life, and in particular the right to a religious training and education; the right to worship God, both in private and in public, including the right to engage in religious works of charity; the right, in principle, to marriage and to the attainment of the purpose of marriage, the right to wedded society and home life; the right to work, as an indispensable means for the maintenance of family life; the right to the free choice of a state of life, and therefore of the priestly and religious state; the right to a use of material goods, subject to its duties and to its social limitations.

ii. *The Protection of Social Unity, and Especially of the Family*

He who would have the star of peace to shine permanently upon society must reject all forms of materialism, which regard the people as nothing but a herd of individuals, disunited and lacking organic cohesion, and as the raw material for domination and arbitrary treatment.

He must endeavour to see society as an organic unity,

growing to maturity under the government of Divine Providence—a unity which, within the spatial limits assigned to it and in the measure of its peculiar endowments, is designed, through the collaboration of the various classes and vocational groups of the community, to achieve the eternal and ever-new ends of culture and religion.

He must defend the indissolubility of marriage. He must give to the family, which is the irreplaceable unit of society, the space, light and air that it needs in order to fulfil its mission of perpetuating new life, and of educating children in a spirit corresponding with its own true religious convictions. He must devote his energies to preserving, protecting, or restoring the economic, spiritual, moral, and juridical unity of the family, by ensuring that the material and spiritual advantages of the family shall be shared also by the domestic staff; by securing for every family a home in which a healthy family life, both physical and moral, may be maintained in all its vigour and dignity; by ensuring that home and place of work are not so distant from each other that the head of the family, the educator of his children, becomes almost a stranger in his own home; by ensuring, above all, that between school and family that bond of confidence and mutual assistance shall be restored which in times past produced such happy results, but which today has given place to mistrust, in cases where the school, under the influence or the control of a materialistic spirit, contaminates and corrupts the good which the parents have instilled into the minds of their children.

iii. *The Dignity and Prerogatives of Labour*

He who would have the star of peace to shine permanently over society must give to labour the place assigned to it by God from the beginning. All labour, as an indispensable means to the mastery of the earth, by which God wills to be glorified, has an inalienable dignity and at the same time an intimate connection with the development of the human person; nor does this noble dignity and prerogative of labour suffer any diminution from the burden of fatigue which, in consequence of original sin, must be endured in obedient submission to the will of God.

Those who are familiar with the great encyclicals of Our Predecessors and with Our own previous messages will know that the Church does not hesitate to draw the practical conclusions which follow from the moral dignity of labour, or to give them the full weight of her authority. The dignity of labour demands not only a just wage, adequate to the needs of the worker and his family, but also the maintenance and development of a social order which will render possible and secure a portion of private property, however modest, for all sections of the community; which will favour a higher education for children of the working classes who are exceptionally intelligent and well-disposed; and which will promote and give effect to a practical social spirit in the neighbourhood, in the district, and throughout the nation, thus mitigating hostility between various classes and interests, and giving to the workers, instead of a feeling of isolation from their fellow men, the comforting experience of a truly human solidarity and Christian brotherhood.

The progress and extent of social reform will depend upon the economic power of each nation. It is only by a rational and generous exchange of resources between the strong nations and the weak that a state of world-wide peace will become possible, and all centres of conflagration and infection, which might give rise to new conflicts, be eliminated.

There are clear signs which lead Us to think that, amidst the ferment of prejudice and hate which are an inevitable but unhappy feature of the war mentality, peoples have not lost the consciousness of their intimate dependence upon one another for good or for ill; indeed, that consciousness appears to have become even more lively and active. Is it not true that serious thinkers are coming to perceive more and more clearly that the way to world salvation lies in the renunciation of national egoism and isolation, ready as they are to ask their own people to bear a heavy burden of the sacrifices which will be needful to bring social peace to other nations? May this Christmas message of Ours, addressed to all men of good will and generous heart, encourage and increase the army of social crusaders in every land! And may God grant to their peaceloving cause the victory which such a noble enterprise deserves!

iv. *The Restoration of the Juridical Order*

He who would have the star of peace to shine permanently over social life must make every effort towards the restoration of a juridical constitution.

The modern idea of justice is often corrupted by a positivist and utilitarian theory and practice subservient to the interests of particular groups, sections, and movements—the course of legislation and the administration of justice being dictated by their policies.

This state of affairs can be remedied only by awakening the human conscience to the need of a juridical constitution based upon God's sovereign lordship and immune from human caprice, a constitution which will use its coercive authority to protect the inviolable rights of man against the aggression of any human power.

A constitution conformable with the divine will gives man a right to juridical security, and accordingly grants him a sphere of rights immune from all arbitrary attack.

The relation of man towards man, of individual towards society and authority and civic duties, and the relation of society and authority towards individuals—all these must be based upon a clear juridical foundation and, where necessary, protected by the authority of the courts. This supposes:

(a) a tribunal and a judge taking their directions from law clearly defined;

(b) clear legal principles which cannot be upset by unwarranted appeals to a supposed popular sentiment or by merely utilitarian considerations;

(c) the recognition of the principle that the State also, and the officials and organizations dependent upon the State, are under the obligation of revising and withdrawing such measures as are incompatible with the liberty, the property, the honour, the advancement, or the welfare of individuals.

v. *The Christian Conception of the State*

He who would have the star of peace to shine permanently upon human society must strive for the recognition of a political theory and practice based upon rational discipline, noble humanity, and a responsible Christian spirit.

He must assist in bringing back the State and the power of the State to its proper function of serving society, and to a full respect for the human person and for his activity in pursuit of his eternal destiny.

He must use every effort to stamp out the errors which cause the State and its authority to depart from the path of moral rectitude, repudiating as it does the eminently ethical bond which connects them with individual and social life and denying or in practice ignoring their essential dependence upon the will of the Creator.

He must promote the general recognition of the truth that, even in the temporal order, the deepest meaning, the ultimate moral basis, and the universal legitimacy of the right to govern, lies in the duty to serve.

✿   ✿   ✿

CHARTER OF THE UNITED NATIONS

★★

WE, THE PEOPLES OF THE UNITED NATIONS, DETER-mined to save succeeding generations from the scourge of war, which twice in our lifetime has brought untold sorrow to mankind, and to reaffirm faith in fundamental human rights, in the dignity and worth of the human person, in the equal rights of men and women and of nations large and small, and

to establish conditions under which justice and respect for the obligations arising from treaties and other sources of international law can be maintained, and

to promote social progress and better standards of life in larger freedom,

AND FOR THESE ENDS

to practice tolerance and live together in peace with one another as good neighbours, and

to unite our strength to maintain international peace and security, and

to ensure, by the acceptance of principles and the institution of methods, that armed force shall not be used, save in the common interests, and

to employ international machinery for the promotion of the economic and social advancement of all peoples,

HAVE RESOLVED TO COMBINE OUR EFFORTS TO AC-
COMPLISH THESE AIMS

Accordingly, our respective Governments, through
representatives assembled in the city of San Francisco,
who have exhibited their full powers found to be in good
and due form, have agreed to the present Charter of the
United Nations and do hereby establish an international
organization to be known as the United Nations.

CHAPTER I

PURPOSES AND PRINCIPLES

Article 1

The Purposes of the United Nations are:

1. To maintain international peace and security, and
to that end: to take effective collective measures for the
prevention and removal of threats to the peace, and for
the suppression of acts of aggression or other breaches of
the peace, and to bring about by peaceful means, and in
conformity with the principles of justice and international
law, adjustment or settlement of international disputes
or situations which might lead to a breach of the peace;

2. To develop friendly relations among nations based
on respect for the principle of equal rights and self-determination of peoples, and to take other appropriate
measures to strengthen universal peace;

3. To achieve international co-operation in solving international problems of an economic, social, cultural, or
humanitarian character, and in promoting and encourag-
ing respect for human rights and for fundamental freedoms for all without distinction as to race, sex, language,
or religion; and

4. To be a centre for harmonizing the actions of nations in the attainment of these common ends.

Article 2

The Organization and its Members, in pursuit of the Purposes stated in Article 1, shall act in accordance with the following Principles.

1. The Organization is based on the principle of the sovereign equality of all its Members.

2. All Members, in order to insure to all of them the rights and benefits resulting from membership, shall fulfil in good faith the obligations assumed by them in accordance with the present Charter.

3. All Members shall settle their international disputes by peaceful means in such a manner that international peace and security, and justice, are not endangered.

4. All Members shall refrain in their international relations from the threat or use of force against the territorial integrity or political independence of any state, or in any other manner inconsistent with the Purposes of the United Nations.

5. All Members shall give the United Nations every assistance in any action it takes in accordance with the present Charter, and shall refrain from giving assistance to any state against which the United Nations is taking preventive or enforcement action.

6. The Organization shall ensure that states which are not Members of the United Nations act in accordance with these Principles so far as may be necessary for the maintenance of international peace and security.

7. Nothing contained in the present Charter shall authorize the United Nations to intervene in matters which are essentially within the domestic jurisdiction of any state or shall require the Members to submit such

matters to settlement under the present Charter; but this principle shall not prejudice the application of enforcement measures under Chapter VII.

CHAPTER II

MEMBERSHIP

Article 3

The original Members of the United Nations shall be the states which, having participated in the United Nations Conference on International Organization at San Francisco, or having previously signed the Declaration by United Nations of January 1, 1942, sign the present Charter and ratify it in accordance with Article 110.

Article 4

1. Membership in the United Nations is open to all other peace-loving states which accept the obligations contained in the present Charter and, in the judgment of the Organization, are able and willing to carry out these obligations.

2. The admission of any such state to membership in the United Nations will be effected by a decision of the General Assembly upon the recommendation of the Security Council.

Article 5

A Member of the United Nations against which preventive or enforcement action has been taken by the Security Council may be suspended from the exercise of the rights and privileges of membership by the General Assembly upon the recommendation of the Security Council. The exercise of these rights and privileges may be restored by the Security Council.

Article 6

A Member of the United Nations which has persistently violated the Principles contained in the present Charter may be expelled from the Organization by the General Assembly upon the recommendation of the Security Council.

CHAPTER III

ORGANS

Article 7

1. There are established as the principal organs of the United Nations: a General Assembly, a Security Council, an Economic and Social Council, a Trusteeship Council, an International Court of Justice, and a Secretariat.

2. Such subsidiary organs as may be found necessary may be established in accordance with the present Charter.

Article 8

The United Nations shall place no restrictions on the eligibility of men and women to participate in any capacity and under conditions of equality in its principal and subsidiary organs.

CHAPTER IV

THE GENERAL ASSEMBLY

Composition

Article 9

1. The General Assembly shall consist of all the Members of the United Nations.

2. Each Member shall have not more than five representatives in the General Assembly.

Functions and Powers

Article 10

The General Assembly may discuss any questions or any matters within the scope of the present Charter or relating to the powers and functions of any organs provided for in the present Charter, and, except as provided in Article 12, may make recommendations to the Members of the United Nations or to the Security Council or to both on any such questions or matters.

Article 11

1. The General Assembly may consider the general principles of co-operation in the maintenance of international peace and security, including the principles governing disarmament and the regulation of armaments, and may make recommendations with regard to such principles to the Members or to the Security Council or to both.

2. The General Assembly may discuss any questions relating to the maintenance of international peace and security brought before it by any Member of the United Nations, or by the Security Council, or by a state which is not a Member of the United Nations in accordance with Article 35, paragraph 2, and, except as provided in Article 12, may make recommendations with regard to any such questions to the state or states concerned or to the Security Council or to both. Any such question on which action is necessary shall be referred to the Security Council by the General Assembly either before or after discussion.

3. The General Assembly may call the attention of the Security Council to situations which are likely to endanger international peace and security.

4. The powers of the General Assembly set forth in this Article shall not limit the general scope of Article 10.

Article 12

1. While the Security Council is exercising in respect of any dispute or situation the functions assigned to it in the present Charter, the General Assembly shall not make any recommendation with regard to that dispute or situation unless the Security Council so requests.

2. The Secretary-General, with the consent of the Security Council, shall notify the General Assembly at each session of any matters relative to the maintenance of international peace and security which are being dealt with by the Security Council and shall similarly notify the General Assembly, or the members of the United Nations if the General Assembly is not in session, immediately the Security Council ceases to deal with such matters.

Article 13

1. The General Assembly shall initiate studies and make recommendations for the purpose of:

> (a) promoting international co-operation in the political field and encouraging the progressive development of international law and its codification;
>
> (b) promoting international co-operation in the economic, social, cultural, educational, and health fields, and assisting in the realization of human rights and fundamental freedoms for all without distinction as to race, sex, language, or religion.

2. The further responsibilities, functions, and powers of

the General Assembly with respect to matters mentioned in paragraph 1 (b) above are set forth in Chapters IX and X.

Article 14

Subject to the provisions of Article 12, the General Assembly may recommend measures for the peaceful adjustment of any situation, regardless of origin, which it deems likely to impair the general welfare or friendly relations among nations, including situations resulting from a violation of the provisions of the present Charter setting forth the Purposes and Principles of the United Nations.

Article 15

1. The General Assembly shall receive and consider annual and special reports from the Security Council; these reports shall include an account of the measures that the Security Council has decided upon or taken to maintain international peace and security.

2. The General Assembly shall receive and consider reports from the other organs of the United Nations.

Article 16

The General Assembly shall perform such functions with respect to the international trusteeship system as are assigned to it under Chapters XII and XIII, including the approval of the trusteeship agreements for areas not designated as strategic.

Article 17

1. The General Assembly shall consider and approve the budget of the Organization.

2. The expenses of the Organization shall be borne by

the Members as apportioned by the General Assembly.

3. The General Assembly shall consider and approve any financial and budgetary arrangements with specialized agencies referred to in Article 57 and shall examine the administrative budgets of such specialized agencies with a view to making recommendations to the agencies concerned.

Voting

Article 18

1. Each member of the General Assembly shall have one vote.

2. Decisions of the General Assembly on important questions shall be made by a two-thirds majority of the members present and voting. These questions shall include: recommendations with respect to the maintenance of international peace and security, the election of the non-permanent members of the Security Council, the election of the members of the Economic and Social Council, the election of members of the Trusteeship Council in accordance with paragraph 1 (c) of Article 86, the admission of new Members to the United Nations, the suspension of the rights and privileges of membership, the expulsion of Members, questions relating to the operation of the trusteeship system, and budgetary questions.

3. Decisions on other questions, including the determination of additional categories of questions to be decided by a two-thirds majority, shall be made by a majority of the members present and voting.

Article 19

A Member of the United Nations which is in arrears in the payment of its financial contributions of the Organization shall have no vote in the General Assembly if the amount of its arrears equals or exceeds the amount of the contributions due from it for the preceding two full years. The General Assembly may, nevertheless, permit such a Member to vote if it is satisfied that the failure to pay is due to conditions beyond the control of the Member.

Procedure

Article 20

The General Assembly shall meet in regular annual sessions and in such special sessions as occasion may require. Special sessions shall be convoked by the Secretary-General at the request of the Security Council or of a majority of the Members of the United Nations.

Article 21

The General Assembly shall adopt its own rules of procedure. It shall elect its President for each session.

Article 22

The General Assembly may establish such subsidiary organs as it deems necessary for the performance of its functions.

CHAPTER V

THE SECURITY COUNCIL

Composition

Article 23

1. The Security Council shall consist of eleven Members of the United Nations. The Republic of China, France, the Union of Soviet Socialist Republics, the

United Kingdom of Great Britain and Northern Ireland, and the United States of America shall be permanent members of the Security Council. The General Assembly shall elect six other Members of the United Nations to be non-permanent members of the Security Council, due regard being specially paid, in the first instance to the contribution of Members of the United Nations to the maintenance of international peace and security and to the other purposes of the Organization, and also to equitable geographical distribution.

2. The non-permanent members of the Security Council shall be elected for a term of two years. In the first election of the non-permanent members, however, three shall be chosen for a term of one year. A retiring member shall not be eligible for immediate re-election.

3. Each member of the Security Council shall have one representative.

Functions and Powers

Article 24

1. In order to ensure prompt and effective action by the United Nations, its Members confer on the Security Council primary responsibility for the maintenance of international peace and security, and agree that in carrying out its duties under this responsibility the Security Council acts on their behalf.

2. In discharging these duties the Security Council shall act in accordance with the Purposes and Principles of the United Nations. The specific powers granted to the Security Council for the discharge of these duties are laid down in Chapters VI, VII, VIII and XII.

3. The Security Council shall submit annual and, when

necessary, special reports to the General Assembly for its consideration.

Article 25

The Members of the United Nations agree to accept and carry out the decisions of the Security Council in accordance with the present Charter.

Article 26

In order to promote the establishment and maintenance of international peace and security with the least diversion for armaments of the world's human and economic resources, the Security Council shall be responsible for formulating, with the assistance of the Military Staff Committee referred to in Article 47, plans to be submitted to the Members of the United Nations for the establishment of a system for the regulation of armaments.

Voting

Article 27

1. Each member of the Security Council shall have one vote.

2. Decisions of the Security Council on procedural matters shall be made by an affirmative vote of seven members.

3. Decisions of the Security Council on all other matters shall be made by an affirmative vote of seven members; including the concurring votes of the permanent members; provided that, in decisions under Chapter VI and under paragraph 3 of Article 52, a party to a dispute shall abstain from voting.

Procedure

Article 28

1. The Security Council shall be so organized as to be able to function continuously. Each member of the Security Council shall for this purpose be represented at all times at the seat of the Organization.

2. The Security Council shall hold periodic meetings at which each of its members may, if it so desires, be represented by a member of the government or by some other specially designated representative.

3. The Security Council may hold meetings at such places other than the seat of the Organization as in its judgment will best facilitate its work.

Article 29

The Security Council may establish such subsidiary organs as it deems necessary for the performance of its functions.

Article 30

The Security Council shall adopt its own rules of procedure, including the method of selecting its President.

Article 31

Any Member of the United Nations which is not a member of the Security Council may participate, without vote, in the discussion of any question brought before the Security Council whenever the latter considers that the interests of that Member are specially affected.

Article 32

Any Member of the United Nations which is not a member of the Security Council or any state which is not a Member of the United Nations, if it is a party to a dispute under consideration by the Security Council, shall be invited to participate, without vote, in the discussion relating to the dispute. The Security Council shall lay down such conditions as it deems just for the participation of a state which is not a Member of the United Nations.

CHAPTER VI

PACIFIC SETTLEMENT OF DISPUTES

Article 33

1. The parties to any dispute, the continuance of which is likely to endanger the maintenance of international peace and security, shall, first of all, seek a solution by negotiation, inquiry, mediation, conciliation, arbitration, judicial settlement, resort to regional agencies or arrangements, or other peaceful means of their own choice.

2. The Security Council shall, when it deems necessary, call upon the parties to settle their dispute by such means.

Article 34

The Security Council may investigate any dispute, or any situation which might lead to international friction or give rise to a dispute, in order to determine whether the continuance of the dispute or situation is likely to endanger the maintenance of international peace and security.

Article 35

1. Any Member of the United Nations may bring any dispute or any situation of the nature referred to in Article 34, to the attention of the Security Council or of the General Assembly.

2. A state which is not a Member of the United Nations may bring to the attention of the Security Council or of

the General Assembly any dispute to which it is a party, if it accepts in advance, for the purposes of the dispute, the obligations of pacific settlement provided in the present Charter.

3. The proceedings of the General Assembly in respect of matters brought to its attention under this Article will be subject to the provisions of Articles 11 and 12.

Article 36

1. The Security Council may, at any stage of a dispute of the nature referred to in Article 33 or of a situation of like nature, recommend appropriate procedures or methods of adjustment.

2. The Security Council should take into consideration any procedures for the settlement of the dispute which have already been adopted by the parties.

3. In making recommendations under this Article the Security Council should also take into consideration that legal disputes should as a general rule be referred by the parties to the International Court of Justice in accordance with the provisions of the Statute of the Court.

Article 37

1. Should the parties to a dispute of the nature referred to in Article 33 fail to settle it by the means indicated in that Article, they shall refer it to the Security Council.

2. If the Security Council deems that the continuance of the dispute is in fact likely to endanger the maintenance of international peace and security, it shall decide whether to take action under Article 36 or to recommend such terms of settlement as it may consider appropriate.

Article 38

Without prejudice to the provisions of Articles 33 to 37 the Security Council may, if all the parties to any dispute so request, make recommendations to the parties with a view to a pacific settlement of the dispute.

CHAPTER VII

ACTION WITH RESPECT TO THREATS TO THE PEACE, BREACHES OF THE PEACE, AND ACTS OF AGGRESSION

Article 39

The Security Council shall determine the existence of any threat to the peace, breach of the peace, or act of aggression and shall make recommendations, or decide what measures shall be taken in accordance with Articles 41 and 42, to maintain or restore international peace and security.

Article 40

In order to prevent an aggravation of the situation, the Security Council may, before making the recommendations or deciding upon the measures provided for in Article 39, call upon the parties concerned to comply with such provisional measures as it deems necessary or desirable. Such provisional measures shall be without prejudice to the rights, claims, or position of the parties concerned. The Security Council shall duly take account of failure to comply with such provisional measures.

Article 41

The Security Council may decide what measures not involving the use of armed force are to be employed to give effect to its decisions, and it may call upon the Members of the United Nations to apply such measures. These may include complete or partial interruption of economic relations and of rail, sea, air, postal, telegraphic, radio, and other means of communication, and the severance of diplomatic relations.

Article 42

Should the Security Council consider that measures provided for in Article 41 would be inadequate or have proved to be inadequate, it may take such action by air, sea, or land forces as may be necessary to maintain or restore international peace and security. Such action may include demonstrations, blockade, and other operations by air, sea, or land forces of Members of the United Nations.

Article 43

1. All Members of the United Nations, in order to contribute to the maintenance of international peace and security, undertake to make available to the Security Council, on its call and in accordance with a special agreement or agreements, armed forces, assistance, and facilities, including rights of passage, necessary for the purpose of maintaining international peace and security.

2. Such agreement or agreements shall govern the numbers and types of forces, their degree of readiness and general location, and the nature of the facilities and assistance to be provided.

3. The agreement or agreements shall be negotiated as soon as possible on the initiative of the Security Council. They shall be concluded between the Security Council and Members or between the Security Council and groups of Members and shall be subject to ratification by the signatory states in accordance with their constitutional processes.

Article 44

When the Security Council has decided to use force it shall, before calling upon a Member not represented on it to provide armed forces in fulfilment of the obligations assumed under Article 43, invite that Member, if the Member so desires, to participate in the decisions of the Security Council concerning the employment of contingents of that Member's armed forces.

Article 45

In order to enable the United Nations to take urgent military measures, Members shall hold immediately available national air-force contingents for combined international enforcement action. The strength and degree of readiness of these contingents and plans for their combined action shall be determined, with the limits laid down in the special agreement or agreements referred to in Article 43, by the Security Council with the assistance of the Military Staff Committee.

Article 46

Plans for the application of armed force shall be made by the Security Council with the assistance of the Military Committee.

Article 47

1. There shall be established a Military Staff Committee to advise and assist the Security Council on all questions relating to the Security Council's military requirements for the maintenance of international peace and security, the employment and command of forces placed at its disposal, the regulation of armaments, and possible disarmament.

2. The Military Staff Committee shall consist of the Chiefs of Staff of the permanent members of the Security Council or their representatives. Any Member of the United Nations not permanently represented on the Committee shall be invited by the Committee to be associated with it when the efficient discharge of the Committee's responsibilities requires the participation of that Member in its work.

3. The Military Staff Committee shall be responsible under the Security Council for the strategic direction of any armed forces placed at the disposal of the Security Council. Questions relating to the command of such forces shall be worked out subsequently.

4. The Military Staff Committee, with the authorization of the Security Council and after consultation with appropriate regional agencies, may establish regional subcommittees.

Article 48

1. The action required to carry out the decisions of the Security Council for the maintenance of international peace and security shall be taken by all the Members of the United Nations or by some of them, as the Security Council may determine.

2. Such decisions shall be carried out by the Members of the United Nations directly and through their action in the appropriate international agencies of which they are members.

Article 49

The Members of the United Nations shall join in affording mutual assistance in carrying out the measures decided upon by the Security Council.

Article 50

If preventive or enforcement measures against any state are taken by the Security Council, any other state, whether a Member of the United Nations or not, which finds itself confronted with special economic problems arising from the carrying out of those measures shall have the right to consult the Security Council with regard to a solution of those problems.

Article 51

Nothing in the present Charter shall impair the inherent right of individual or collective self-defence if an armed attack occurs against a Member of the United Nations, until the Security Council has taken the measures necessary to maintain international peace and security. Measures taken by Members in the exercise of this right of self-defence shall be immediately reported to the Security Council and shall not in any way affect the authority and responsibility of the Security Council under the present Charter to take at any time such action as it deems necessary in order to maintain or restore international peace and security.

CHAPTER VIII

REGIONAL ARRANGEMENTS

Article 52

1. Nothing in the present Charter precludes the existence of regional arrangements or agencies for dealing with such matters relating to the maintenance of international peace and security as are appropriate for regional action, provided that such arrangements or agencies and

their activities are consistent with the Purposes and Principles of the United Nations.

2. The Members of the United Nations entering into such arrangements or constituting such agencies shall make every effort to achieve pacific settlement of local disputes through such regional arrangements or by such regional agencies before referring them to the Security Council.

3. The Security Council shall encourage the development of pacific settlement of local disputes through such regional arrangements or by such regional agencies either on the initiative of the states concerned or by reference from the Security Council.

4. This Article in no way impairs the application of Articles 34 and 35.

Article 53

1. The Security Council shall, where appropriate, utilize such regional arrangements or agencies for enforcement action under its authority. But no enforcement action shall be taken under regional arrangements or by regional agencies without the authorization of the Security Council, with the exception of measures against any enemy state, as defined in paragraph 2 of this Article, provided for pursuant to Article 107 or in regional arrangements directed against renewal of aggressive policy on the part of any such state, until such time as the Organization may, on request of the Governments concerned, be charged with the responsibility for preventing further aggression by such a state.

2. The term enemy State as used in paragraph 1 of this Article applies to any state which during the Second World War has been an enemy of any signatory of the present Charter.

Article 54

The Security Council shall at all times be kept fully informed of activities undertaken or in contemplation under regional arrangements or by regional agencies for the maintenance of international peace and security.

CHAPTER IX

INTERNATIONAL ECONOMIC AND SOCIAL CO-OPERATION

Article 55

With a view to the creation of conditions of stability and well-being which are necessary for peaceful and friendly relations among nations based on respect for the principle of equal rights and self-determination of peoples, the United Nations shall promote:

(a) higher standards of living, full employment, and conditions of economic and social progress and development;

(b) solutions of international economic, social, health, and related problems; and international cultural and educational co-operation; and

(c) universal respect for, and observance of, human rights and fundamental freedoms for all without distinction as to race, sex, language, or religion.

Article 56

All Members pledge themselves to take joint and separate action in co-operation with the Organization for the achievement of the purposes set forth in Article 55.

Article 57

1. The various specialized agencies, established by inter-governmental agreement and having wide interna-

tional responsibilities, as defined in their basic instruments, in economic, social, cultural, educational, health, and related fields, shall be brought into relationship with the United Nations in accordance with the provisions of Article 63.

2. Such agencies thus brought into relationship with the United Nations are hereinafter referred to as specialized agencies.

Article 58

The Organization shall make recommendations for the co-ordination of the policies and activities of the specialized agencies.

Article 59

The Organization shall, where appropriate, initiate negotiations among the states concerned for the creation of any new specialized agencies required for the accomplishment of the purposes set forth in Article 55.

Article 60

Responsibility for the discharge of the functions of the Organization set forth in this Chapter shall be vested in the General Assembly and, under the authority of the General Assembly, in the Economic and Social Council, which shall have for this purpose the powers set forth in Chapter X.

CHAPTER X

ECONOMIC AND SOCIAL COUNCIL

Composition

Article 61

1. The Economic and Social Council shall consist of

eighteen members of the United Nations elected by the General Assembly.

2. Subject to the provisions of paragraph 3, six members of the Economic and Social Council shall be elected each year for a term of three years. A retiring member shall be eligible for immediate re-election.

3. At the first election, eighteen members of the Economic and Social Council shall be chosen. The term of office of six members so chosen shall expire at the end of one year, and of six other members at the end of two years, in accordance with arrangements made by the General Assembly.

4. Each member of the Economic and Social Council shall have one representative.

Functions and Powers

Article 62

1. The Economic and Social Council may make or initiate studies and reports with respect to international economic, social, cultural, educational, health, and related matters and may make recommendations with respect to any such matters to the General Assembly, to the Members of the United Nations, and to the specialized agencies concerned.

2. It may make recommendations for the purpose of promoting respect for, and observance of, human rights and fundamental freedoms for all.

3. It may prepare draft conventions for submission to the General Assembly, with respect to matters falling within its competence.

4. It may call, in accordance with the rules prescribed by the United Nations, international conferences on matters falling within its competence.

Article 63

1. The Economic and Social Council may enter into agreements with any of the agencies referred to in Article 57, defining the terms on which the agency concerned shall be brought into relationship with the United Nations. Such agreements shall be subject to approval by the General Assembly.

2. It may co-ordinate the activities of the specialized agencies through consultation with and recommendations to such agencies and through recommendations to the General Assembly and to the Members of the United Nations.

Article 64

1. The Economic and Social Council may take appropriate steps to obtain regular reports from the specialized agencies. It may make arrangements with the Members of the United Nations and with the specialized agencies to obtain reports on the steps taken to give effect to its own recommendations and to recommendations on matters falling within its competence made by the General Assembly.

2. It may communicate its observations on these reports to the General Assembly.

Article 65

The Economic and Social Council may furnish information to the Security Council and shall assist the Security Council upon its request.

Article 66

1. The Economic and Social Council shall perform such functions as fall within its competence in connection with

the carrying out of the recommendations of the General Assembly.

2. It may, with the approval of the General Assembly, perform services at the request of Members of the United Nations and at the request of specialized agencies.

3. It shall perform such other functions as are specified elsewhere in the present Charter or as may be assigned to it by the General Assembly.

Voting

Article 67

1. Each member of the Economic and Social Council shall have one vote.

2. Decisions of the Economic and Social Council shall be made by a majority of the members present and voting.

Procedure

Article 68

The Economic and Social Council shall set up commissions in economic and social fields and for the promotion of human rights, and such other commissions as may be required for the performance of its functions.

Article 69

The Economic and Social Council shall invite any Member of the United Nations to participate, without vote, in its deliberations on any matter of particular concern to that Member.

Article 70

The Economic and Social Council may make arrangements for representatives of the specialized agencies to participate, without vote, in its deliberations and in those of the commissions established by it, and for its representatives to participate in the deliberations of the specialized agencies.

Article 71

The Economic and Social Council may make suitable arrangements for consultation with non-governmental organizations which are concerned with matters within its competence. Such arrangements may be made with international organizations and, where appropriate, with national organizations after consultation with the Member of the United Nations concerned.

Article 72

1. The Economic and Social Council shall adopt its own rules of procedure, including the method of selecting its President.

2. The Economic and Social Council shall meet as required in accordance with its rules, which shall include provision for the convening of meetings on the request of a majority of its members.

CHAPTER XI

DECLARATION REGARDING NON-SELF-GOVERNING TERRITORIES

Article 73

Members of the United Nations which have or assume responsibilities for the administration of territories whose peoples have not yet attained a full measure of self-government recognize the principle that the interests of the inhabitants of these territories are paramount, and accept as a sacred trust the obligation to promote to the

227

utmost within the system of international peace and security established by the present Charter, the well-being of the inhabitants of these territories, and, to this end:

(a) to ensure, with due respect for the culture of the peoples concerned, their political, economic, social, and educational advancement, their just treatment, and their protection against abuses;

(b) to develop self-government, to take due account of the political aspirations of the peoples, and to assist them in the progressive development of their free political institutions, according to the particular circumstances of each territory and its peoples and their varying stages of advancement;

(c) to further international peace and security;

(d) to promote constructive measures of development, to encourage research, and to co-operate with one another and, when and where appropriate, with specialized international bodies with a view to the practical achievement of the social, economic, and scientific purposes set forth in this Article; and

(e) to transmit regularly to the Secretary-General for information purposes, subject to such limitation as security and constitutional considerations may require, statistical and other information of a technical nature relating to economic, social, and educational conditions in the territories for which they are respectively responsible other than those territories to which Chapters XII and XIII apply.

Article 74

Members of the United Nations also agree that their policy in respect of the territories to which this Chapter applies, no less than in respect of their metropolitan areas,

must be based on the general principle of good-neighbour-
liness, due account being taken of the interests and well-
being of the rest of the world, in social, economic, and
commercial matters.

CHAPTER XII

INTERNATIONAL TRUSTEESHIP SYSTEM

Article 75

The United Nations shall establish under its authority
an international trusteeship system for the administration
and supervision of such territories as may be placed
thereunder by subsequent individual agreements. These
territories are hereinafter referred to as trust territories.

Article 76

The basic objectives of the trusteeship system, in accordance with the Purposes of the United Nations laid
down in Article 1 of the present Charter, shall be:

(a) to further international peace and security;

(b) to promote the political, economic, social, and
educational advancement of the inhabitants of the
trust territories, and their progressive development
towards self-government or independence as may be
appropriate to the particular circumstances of each
territory and its peoples and the freely expressed
wishes of the peoples concerned, and as may be provided by the terms of each trusteeship agreement;

(c) to encourage respect for human rights and for
fundamental freedoms for all without distinction as
to race, sex, language, or religion, and to encourage
recognition of the interdependence of the peoples of
the world; and

(d) to ensure equal treatment in social, economic, and commercial matters for all Members of the United Nations and their nationals, and also equal treatment for the latter in the administration of justice, without prejudice to the attainment of the foregoing objectives and subject to the provisions of Article 80.

Article 77

1. The trusteeship system shall apply to such territories in the following categories as may be placed thereunder by means of trusteeship agreements:

(a) territories now held under mandate;

(b) territories which may be detached from enemy states as a result of the Second World War; and

(c) territories voluntarily placed under the system by states responsible for their administration.

2. It will be a matter for subsequent agreement as to which territories in the foregoing categories will be brought under the trusteeship system and upon what terms.

Article 78

The trusteeship system shall not apply to territories which have become Members of the United Nations, relationship among which shall be based on respect for the principle of sovereign equality.

Article 79

The terms of trusteeship for each territory to be placed under the trusteeship system, including any alteration or amendment, shall be agreed upon by the states directly concerned, including the mandatory power in the case of territories held under mandate by a Member of the United Nations, and shall be approved as provided for in Articles 83 and 85.

Article 80

1. Except as may be agreed upon in individual trusteeship agreements, made under Articles 77, 79, and 81, placing each territory under the trusteeship system, and until such agreements have been concluded, nothing in this Chapter shall be construed in or of itself to alter in any manner the rights whatsoever of any states or any peoples or the terms of existing international instruments to which Members of the United Nations may respectively be parties.

2. Paragraph 1 of this Article shall not be interpreted as giving grounds for delay or postponement of the negotiation and conclusion of agreements for placing mandated and other territories under the trusteeship system as provided for in Article 77.

Article 81

The trusteeship agreement shall in each case include the terms under which the trust territory will be administered and designate the authority which will exercise the administration of the trust territory. Such authority, hereinafter called the administering authority, may be one or more states or the Organization itself.

Article 82

There may be designated, in any trusteeship agreement, a strategic area or areas which may include part or all of the trust territory to which the agreement applies, without prejudice to any special agreement or agreements made under Article 43.

Article 83

1. All functions of the United Nations relating to strategic areas, including the approval of the terms of the trusteeship agreements and of their alteration or amendment, shall be exercised by the Security Council.

2. The basic objectives set forth in Article 76 shall be applicable to the people of each strategic area.

3. The Security Council shall, subject to the provisions of the trusteeship agreements and without prejudice to security considerations, avail itself of the assistance of the Trusteeship Council to perform those functions of the United Nations under the trusteeship system relating to political, economic, social, and educational matters in the strategic areas.

Article 84

It shall be the duty of the administering authority to ensure that the trust territory shall play its part in the maintenance of international peace and security. To this end the administering authority may make use of volunteer forces, facilities, and assistance from the trust territory in carrying out the obligations towards the Security Council undertaken in this regard by the administering authority, as well as for local defence and the maintenance of law and order within the trust territory.

Article 85

1. The functions of the United Nations with regard to trusteeship agreements for all areas not designated as strategic, including the approval of the terms of the trusteeship agreements and of their alteration or amend-

ment, shall be exercised by the General Assembly.

2. The Trusteeship Council, operating under the authority of the General Assembly, shall assist the General Assembly in carrying out these functions.

CHAPTER XIII

THE TRUSTEESHIP COUNCIL

Composition

Article 86

1. The Trusteeship Council shall consist of the following Members of the United Nations:

(a) those Members administering trust territories;

(b) such of those Members mentioned by name in Article 23 as are not administering trust territories; and

(c) as many other Members elected for three-year terms by the General Assembly as may be necessary to ensure that the total number of members of the Trusteeship Council is equally divided between those Members of the United Nations which administer trust territories and those which do not.

2. Each member of the Trusteeship Council shall designate one specially qualified person to represent it therein.

Functions and Powers

Article 87

The General Assembly and, under its authority, the Trusteeship Council, in carrying out their functions, may:

(a) consider reports submitted by the administering authority;

(b) accept petitions and examine them in consultation with the administering authority;

(c) provide for periodic visits to the respective trust territories at times agreed upon with the administering authority; and

(d) take these and other actions in conformity with the terms of the trusteeship agreements.

Article 88

The Trusteeship Council shall formulate a questionnaire on the political, economic, social, and educational advancement of the inhabitants of each trust territory, and the administering authority for each trust territory within the competence of the General Assembly shall make an annual report to the General Assembly upon the basis of such a questionnaire.

Voting

Article 89

1. Each member of the Trusteeship Council shall have one vote.

2. Decisions of the Trusteeship Council shall be made by a majority of the members present and voting.

Procedure

Article 90

1. The Trusteeship Council shall adopt its own rules of procedure, including the method of selecting its President.

2. The Trusteeship Council shall meet as required in accordance with its rules, which shall include provision for the convening of meetings on the request of a majority of its members.

Article 91

The Trusteeship Council shall, when appropriate, avail itself of the assistance of the Economic and Social Council and of the specialized agencies in regard to matters with which they are respectively concerned.

CHAPTER XIV

THE INTERNATIONAL COURT OF JUSTICE

Article 92

The International Court of Justice shall be the principal judicial organ of the United Nations. It shall function in accordance with the annexed Statute, which is based upon the Statute of the Permanent Court of International Justice and forms an integral part of the present Charter.

Article 93

1. All Members of the United Nations are *ipso facto* parties to the Statute of the International Court of Justice.

2. A state which is not a Member of the United Nations may become a party to the Statute of the International Court of Justice on conditions to be determined in each case by the General Assembly upon the recommendation of the Security Council.

Article 94

1. Each Member of the United Nations undertakes to comply with the decision of the International Court of Justice in any case to which it is a party.

2. If any party to a case fails to perform the obligations incumbent upon it under a judgment rendered by the Court, the other party may have recourse to the Security Council, which may, if it deems necessary, make recom-

mendations or decide upon measures to be taken to give effect to the judgment.

Article 95

Nothing in the present Charter shall prevent Members of the United Nations from entrusting the solution of their differences to other tribunals by virtue of agreements already in existence or which may be concluded in the future.

Article 96

1. The General Assembly or the Security Council may request the International Court of Justice to give an advisory opinion on any legal question.

2. Other organs of the United Nations and specialized agencies, which may at any time be so authorized by the General Assembly, may also request advisory opinions of the Court on legal questions arising within the scope of their activities.

CHAPTER XV

THE SECRETARIAT

Article 97

The Secretariat shall comprise a Secretary-General and such staff as the Organization may require. The Secretary-General shall be appointed by the General Assembly upon the recommendation of the Security Council. He shall be the chief administrative officer of the Organization.

Article 98

The Secretary-General shall act in that capacity in all meetings of the General Assembly, of the Security Council, of the Economic and Social Council, and of the Trusteeship Council, and shall perform such other functions as are entrusted to him by these organs. The Secretary-General shall make an annual report to the General Assembly on the work of the Organization.

Article 99

The Secretary-General may bring to the attention of the Security Council any matter which in his opinion may threaten the maintenance of international peace and security.

Article 100

1. In the performance of their duties the Secretary-General and the staff shall not seek or receive instructions from any government or from any other authority external to the Organization. They shall refrain from any action which might reflect on their position as international officials responsible only to the Organization.

2. Each Member of the United Nations undertakes to respect the exclusively international character of the responsibilities of the Secretary-General and the staff and not to seek to influence them in the discharge of their responsibilities.

Article 101

1. The staff shall be appointed by the Secretary-General under regulations established by the General Assembly.

2. Appropriate staffs shall be permanently assigned to the Economic and Social Council, the Trusteeship Council, and, as required, to other organs of the United Nations. These staffs shall form a part of the Secretariat.

3. The paramount consideration in the employment of the staff and in the determination of the conditions of

service shall be the necessity of securing the highest standards of efficiency, competence, and integrity. Due regard shall be paid to the importance of recruiting the staff on as wide a geographical basis as possible.

CHAPTER XVI

MISCELLANEOUS PROVISIONS

Article 102

1. Every treaty and every international agreement entered into by any Member of the United Nations after the present Charter comes into force shall as soon as possible be registered with the Secretariat and published by it.

2. No party to any such treaty or international agreement which has not been registered in accordance with the provisions of paragraph 1 of this Article may invoke that treaty or agreement before any organ of the United Nations.

Article 103

In the event of a conflict between the obligations of the Members of the United Nations under the present Charter and their obligations under any other international agreement, their obligations under the present Charter shall prevail.

Article 104

The Organization shall enjoy in the territory of each of its Members such legal capacity as may be necessary for the exercise of its functions and the fulfilment of its purposes.

Article 105

1. The Organization shall enjoy in the territory of each

of its Members such privileges and immunities as are necessary for the fulfilment of its purposes.

2. Representatives of the Members of the United Nations and officials of the Organization shall similarly enjoy such privileges and immunities as are necessary for the independent exercise of their functions in connexion with the Organization.

3. The General Assembly may make recommendations with a view to determining the details of the application of paragraphs 1 and 2 of this Article or may propose conventions to the Members of the United Nations for this purpose.

CHAPTER XVII

TRANSITIONAL SECURITY ARRANGEMENTS

Article 106

Pending the coming into force of such special agreements referred to in Article 43 as in the opinion of the Security Council enable it to begin the exercise of its responsibilities under Article 42, the parties to the Four-Nation Declaration, signed at Moscow, October 30, 1943, and France, shall, in accordance with the provisions of paragraph 5 of that Declaration, consult with one another and as occasion requires with other Members of the United Nations with a view to such joint action on behalf of the Organization as may be necessary for the purpose of maintaining international peace and security.

Article 107

Nothing in the present Charter shall invalidate or preclude action, in relation to any state which during the Second World War has been an enemy of any signatory to the present Charter, taken or authorized as a result of that war by the Governments having responsibility for such action.

CHAPTER XVIII

AMENDMENTS

Article 108

Amendments to the present Charter shall come into force for all Members of the United Nations when they have been adopted by a vote of two-thirds of the members of the General Assembly and ratified in accordance with their respective constitutional processes by two-thirds of the Members of the United Nations, including all the permanent members of the Security Council.

Article 109

1. A General Conference of the Members of the United Nations for the purpose of reviewing the present Charter may be held at a date and place to be fixed by a two-thirds vote of the members of the General Assembly and by a vote of any seven members of the Security Council. Each Member of the United Nations shall have one vote in the conference.

2. Any alteration of the present Charter recommended by a two-thirds vote of the conference shall take effect when ratified in accordance with their respective constitutional processes by two-thirds of the Members of the United Nations including all the permanent members of the Security Council.

3. If such a conference has not been held before the tenth annual session of the General Assembly following the coming into force of the present Charter, the proposal to call such a conference shall be placed on the agenda of

that session of the General Assembly, and the conference shall be held if so decided by a majority vote of the members of the General Assembly and by a vote of any seven members of the Security Council.

CHAPTER XIX

RATIFICATION AND SIGNATURE

Article 110

1. The present Charter shall be ratified by the signatory states in accordance with their respective constitutional processes.

2. The ratifications shall be deposited with the Government of the United States of America, which shall notify all the signatory states of each deposit as well as the Secretary-General of the Organization when he has been appointed.

3. The present Charter shall come into force upon the deposit of ratifications by the Republic of China, France, the Union of Soviet Socialist Republics, the United Kingdom of Great Britain and Northern Ireland, and the United States of America, and by a majority of the other signatory states. A protocol of the ratifications deposited shall thereupon be drawn up by the Government of the United States of America which shall communicate copies thereof to all the signatory states.

4. The states signatory to the present Charter which ratify it after it has come into force will become original Members of the United Nations on the date of the deposit of their respective ratifications.

Article 111

The present Charter, of which the Chinese, French, Russian, English, and Spanish texts are equally authentic, shall remain deposited in the archives of the Government of the United States of America. Duly certified copies thereof shall be transmitted by that Government to the Governments of the other signatory states.

IN FAITH WHEREOF the representatives of the Governments of the United Nations have signed the present Charter.

DONE at the city of San Francisco the twenty-sixth day of June, one thousand nine hundred and forty-five.

Appendix III

A DECLARATION OF RIGHTS

★★★

DRAFTED BY A COMMITTEE APPOINTED BY THE

NATIONAL CATHOLIC WELFARE CONFERENCE,

FEBRUARY 2, 1947

General Preamble

God, the Creator of the human race, has charged man with obligations arising from his personal dignity, from his immortal destiny, and from his relationships as a social being. These obligations are in reference to the Creator, to himself, to his family and fellowmen, to the State and to the community of States. For the fulfilment of these obligations man is endowed with certain natural, inalienable rights. These obligations and rights form the substance of the natural moral law which can be known by reason.

Obligations and rights are correlative. At all times the obligation to respect the rights of others operates against the arbitrary use of rights.

Suitable opportunity to discharge fundamental obligations in the various and separate situations of life is a right which cannot be justly denied. For man's use God has provided the basic resources of this world.

The unity of the human race under God is not broken by geographical distance or by diversity of civilization, culture and economy, and the adequate use of the world's resources by all peoples is not to be denied because of these factors.

Weakness resulting from conquest or imperfection in governmental organization should not be used as a pretext to reject the fundamental rights of man or to impede their legitimate exercise.

The order of rights outlined below progresses through the individual, the family, the State and the community of States.

PART I

THE RIGHTS OF THE HUMAN PERSON

Preamble

The dignity of man, created in the image of God, obligates him to live in accordance with law imposed by God. Consequently, he is endowed as an individual and as a member of society with rights which are inalienable.

Among these rights are:

(1) The right to life and bodily integrity from the moment of conception, regardless of physical or mental condition, except in just punishment for crime.

(2) The right to serve and worship God in private and in public.

(3) The right to religious formation through education and association.

(4) The right to personal liberty under just law.

(5) The right to the equal protection of just law regardless of sex, nationality, color or creed.

(6) The right to freedom of expression, of information and of communication in accordance with truth and justice.

(7) The right to choose and freely to maintain a state of life, married or single, lay or religious.

(8) The right to education suitable for the maintenance and development of man's dignity as a human person.

(9) The right to petition the government for redress of grievances.

(10) The right to a nationality.

(11) The right of access to the means of livelihood, by migration if necessary.

(12) The right of association and peaceable assembly.

(13) The right to work and choose one's occupation.

(14) The right to personal ownership, use and disposal of property subject to the rights of others and to limitation in the interest of the general welfare.

(15) The right to a living wage.

(16) The right to collective bargaining.

(17) The right to associate by industries and professions to obtain economic justice and the general welfare.

(18) The right to assistance from society, if necessary from the State, in distress of person or family.

PART II

THE RIGHTS PERTAINING TO THE FAMILY

Preamble

The family is the natural and fundamental group unit of society and is endowed by the Creator with inalienable rights antecedent to all positive law. The family does not exist for the State, but on the other hand is not independent.

Among these rights are:

(1) The right to marry, to establish a home and beget children.

(2) The right to economic security sufficient for the stability and independence of the family.

(3) The right to the protection of maternity.

(4) The right to educate the children.

(5) The right to maintain, if necessary by public protection and assistance, adequate standards of child welfare within the family circle.

(6) The right to assistance, through community services in the education and care of the children.

(7) The right to housing adapted to the needs and functions of family life.

(8) The right to immunity of the home from search and trespass.

(9) The right to protection against immoral conditions in the community.

PART III

THE DOMESTIC RIGHTS OF STATES

Preamble

Political authority is entrusted by God to nations, which are endowed with rights and charged with the obligation of establishing justice, of promoting the general welfare of their citizens and of co-operating with other nations in furthering the universal welfare of mankind.

It is the right of all peoples that are capable of self-government to organize politically and to function as States upon equal terms with other States.

Among these rights are:

(1) The right to enact just laws binding in conscience.

(2) The right to establish courts of justice and to enforce the observance of law with adequate sanctions.

(3) The right to demand of its citizens respect for the rights of minorities.

(4) The right to tax by adequate and equitable means in order to carry out its proper functions.

(5) The right to exercise eminent domain when demanded by the common welfare.

(6) The right to require that its people receive an education suitable for citizenship.

(7) The right to defend itself against domestic violence.

(8) The right to watch over, stimulate, restrain and order the private activities of individuals and groups in the degree that is necessary for the common good.

(9) The right to regulate operations of international economic groups functioning within its own boundaries.

(10) The right to adopt in time of emergency special measures necessary for the common good.

PART IV

THE RIGHTS OF STATES IN THE INTERNATIONAL COMMUNITY

Preamble

The human family constitutes an organic unity or a world society.

The States of the world have the right and the duty to

associate and to organize in the international community for their common welfare.

The indispensable foundation of all peaceful intercourse among nations and an essential condition of juridical relations among them are common trust and respect for the plighted word. Treaties and agreements must not be considered subject to arbitrary unilateral repudiation.

Every State has certain fundamental rights in the international community.

Among these rights are:

(1) The right to exist as a member of the international community and to be protected in its national life and integrity against acts of aggression by any other State or States.

(2) The right to independence in the determination of its own domestic and foreign policies in accordance with the principles of morality, and subject to the obligations of international law.

(3) The right to juridical equality with other States in the family of nations.

(4) The right to membership in the organized international community and to the benefits of international co-operation.

(5) The right to the assistance of the international community in securing the fulfilment of the terms of a just treaty or agreement.

(6) The right to obtain from the international community redress of grievances arising from unjust treaties imposed by force.

(7) The right to the revision of treaties which are no longer in accord with fundamental justice.

(8) The right to recourse to the procedures of pacific settlement established by the international community

for disputes which diplomatic negotiations have failed to settle.

(9) The right to maintain political, economic and social intercourse with other States upon equal terms.

(10) The right of access, upon equal terms, to the markets and raw materials of the world necessary for its own life as a people.

(11) The right to protect its own natural resources and economic life from unjust exploitation.

(12) The right to the assistance of the international community in time of economic or social distress.

(13) The right to grant asylum to refugees from injustice.

INDEX

References are to page numbers

✶✶✶

Index

Index

Index

Index

Index

Index

Index